BOMBAY GIN

NAROPA UNIVERSITY
The Jack Kerouac School of Disembodied Poetics

ISBN: 978-0-9835873-3-0

Design and Typesetting: HR Hegnauer
Cover artwork: Olivia Locher

Please see our website for submission guidelines.

Bombay Gin can be purchased at Small Press Distribution, on our website, and at the address below for $12 per issue, plus $3 shipping. Back issues are $8 each, plus $3 shipping. Subscription pricing below includes shipping costs.

Bombay Gin
The Jack Kerouac School of Disembodied Poetics
NAROPA UNIVERSITY
2130 Arapahoe Avenue
Boulder, CO 80302

SUBSCRIPTIONS
Individuals, Institutions & International
One year (two issues): $20
Two years (four issues): $36

For more information, visit *Bombay Gin* at:
http://www.naropa.edu/bombaygin

BOMBAY GIN : VOL. 39, NO. 1

EDITORIAL BOARD AND STAFF

BOMBAY GIN 39:1

CONTENTS

BOOK REVIEWS

LETTER FROM THE EDITOR

When Art and Layout Editor Brenna Lee gave CAConrad a choice between fertility, transgression, and contemplative poetics, CA choose "transgression" and "contemplative poetics." And so the theme of issue 39.1 is "The Contemplative as Transgressive." Actually, the idea originally occurred as I considered a contemplative writing course I was set to teach this fall for the Jack Kerouac School's low-residency MFA program. At the beginning of the summer, I posed it to the 2012-13 *Bombay Gin* board, and, as a thought will, it became spirit and then body. All themed issues are a mix of constraint and spontaneity; the result is a rich interpretation of *Bombay Gin's* unique contemplative heritage. Naropa University was founded in 1974 as the Naropa Institute by Chögyam Trungpa Rinpoche, a lineage holder of both the Kagyü and Nyingma Buddhist traditions. To this day, Naropa identifies itself as a Buddhist-inspired university, committed to integrating the praxis of scholarship and activism with the contemplative life of study and meditative practice. In the Jack Kerouac School in particular, we grapple with how to articulate the synergy between contemplative practice and "radical exploration and experimentation" (as our website boasts).

I think part of this difficulty lies in the necessity to (meta)articulate what is obvious: writing is already a contemplative practice, and, in this way, to write contemplatively requires both innovation and a conscious return to origin, whether this be self or intuition. As Marketing Editor Sally Smith has brought to my attention, "radical" is one of those curious terms that contains in its definition the full range of extremes. Its Latin etymology means, "having roots," while its more recent definition jettisons the term toward "extreme change from accepted or traditional forms." I find this mongrel term especially fitting as a modifier not only because of its inclusion of the whole linear iteration of "exploration and experimentation," but also because of the way that path becomes event, rupturing and redoubling (to use Derrida's description of structuralism).

I suppose I originally proposed "transgressive" to mean something like "radical exertion"—transgression is what happens when the soul heaps "itself on that ridge" of "a self-evolving circle" and then "tends outward with a vast force, and to immense and innumerable expansion," as Emerson writes in the essay "Circles." Western culture often understands the contemplative life as hermetic and isolated, bound, but this issue of *Bombay Gin* indicates that transgression is the inevitable trajectory of awareness. In the introduction to his five poems included in this issue, Reed Bye writes of contemplative poetics, "What is 'transgressed' in such a contemplative approach are all the conceptual reflexes and boundaries mind encounters, beginning with biases toward oneself and extending out to judgments or ideas felt or perceived in the world." Like the term "radical," Reed's insight both introduces and directs this issue of *Bombay Gin*, which, in ways we could have never predicted, follows the mind's emergence from its backgrounds, its conditioning, its habitual responses.

One pattern of note is resonance with existentialism's *pour-soi* or the conscious process of estranging the self from ideology and reification. In addition to CAConrad's insightful interview with Brenna Lee, "(Soma) tic Disobedience," I want to highlight Rebecca Brown's "Transgressive Meditation"; Anna Joy Springer's "Identity as Encounter: I as Thou in Discontinuous Memoir," which directly references the existentialist theologian Martin Buber; Erik Anderson's excerpt from *Estranger*; and Michelle Auerbach's essay on kari edwards, "Can I Do This Spiritual Drag." Interfaith and interdisciplinary, these prose pieces push at boundaries of self, gender, and animal and suggest that while only the individual can do the work of revealing the reality of herself, she cannot access the truth of the self without also seeing herself in context of others.

The lovely "lyric" pieces (both prose and poetry) collected here also evidence this dialectic of self and other, even as that other fades into context of the poetic utterance. Barbara Henning, Mg Roberts, HR

Hegnauer, Chris Martin, and Matthew Cooperman, to name only a few, express "a practice of active attention and direct engagement with things as they arise in perception, thought, or emotion, based in open curiosity and appreciation for experience as a whole," to quote again from Reed Bye. In this same vein, we are also proud to curate two portfolios with art from Olivia Locher (whose photographs are on our cover), Debbie Carlos, and Ian Rummell. In a departure from our typical design, in which the image shares the page with its title and the artist's name, we've allowed these images to saturate their space on the page, to be fully present lyric spaces.

Finally, we close the issue with several "experiments," including CAConrad's "(Soma)tic Exercise: Grave a Hole as Dream a Hole," Angela Stubbs' "Blue Ritual," and Richard Cohen's "Play the Platypus Game." These exercises, rituals, games appropriately close the issue by opening a space for you, reader, to enter. To again quote Reed Bye, "For the creative aspect of making (poetics), anything and everything happens from there."

—J'Lyn Chapman

BOMBAY GIN

REED BYE

CONTEMPLATIVE TRANSGRESSION

With the influx of Asian Buddhist meditative and contemplative teachings in the West in the mid-twentieth century, both the practice of mindfulness-awareness meditation and the Buddhist tradition's psychological maps and insights began to become more available to people in the Americas. At Naropa University, poets who were interested in such practice in its relation to direct perception and spontaneous expression encountered meditation teachers from various Buddhist and other traditions.

One result of this encounter has been the development of what has at times been called a contemplative poetics, or dharma poetics, based in the cultivation of active attention—in body, senses, heart, and intellect—through the foundation practice of mindfulness and awareness meditation. This development can be seen as a natural extension of many of the body-mind-language and identity concerns and investigations of later twentieth- and early twenty-first-century poetics. Here the point is making live contact with one's experience in language and staying with it, rather than jumping into a reactive stance to experience and then using language to justify it.

As Denise Levertov reminds us, to "contemplate" is to stand openly in the presence of the ordinary, "noticing," as Allen Ginsberg aphorized, "what you notice": a way to be alive and relax into the reality of the present while also seeing habits of conceptual grasping and fixating, hope and fear, etc. Contemplative poetics suggests a practice of active attention and direct engagement with things as they arise in perception, thought, or emotion, based in open curiosity and appreciation for experience as a whole. In this engagement, language, spoken or written, is the medium in and through which attention discovers and realizes naturally spontaneous intelligence. What is trained in this practice is the ability to stay on one's toes and be surprised, and say it.

What is "transgressed" in such a contemplative approach are all the conceptual reflexes and boundaries mind encounters, beginning with biases toward oneself and extending out to judgments or ideas felt or perceived in the world. All are equally vulnerable to the penetrating insight of lucid awareness. From this basis, everything, as Chögyam Trungpa might say, becomes "workable." Giving in, you can take it on.

Degrees and kinds of pain and confusion, from existential to autobiographical to political, can be motivators of the poetic act or exploration, as can experiences of joy. Sometimes you don't need any motivation; you just do it. A contemplative approach to poetics enters the act of composition in a way that stays in contact with the energies inside that act, but refrains from the impulse to translate these "first thoughts" into something more processed. There is growing trust that the writing knows what it's doing.

And while people doing contemplative practice may appear to be silent and calm, cultivating such states as the purpose of their practice, on the inside the experience may feel very different. Practice is a kind of engagement in feeling, gaining familiarity with and realizing the nature of immediate experience; all of it. For the creative aspect of making (poetics), anything and everything happens from there.

REED BYE

HOW IT BEGINS, WITH STEPS INTO

The unknown. A thin skin
leads us on, as one who can see the way
a fox does and has felt the wind
collapse his home. What is left?
A length of wire and when that runs out
a tender dream
standing above, breasts bared and
smiling. The sun was sharp
Bits and pieces shared its course
What was then discovered? The job to do
It lit the way
that flowed in currents, adjusting
balances from side to side
How does one get rid of the lumps
with heart of previous day intact
or with a new one starting? Breath anyway
reads the symptoms, makes its diagnosis
and prescribes what truth to take—
Flag begins to flap; spoon stirs; lift to
take it in

THERE IN THE THROAT AS IT TURNS

Among lights, forcing obvious spectacles
higher up the nose, cantilevered
re-boxed, and hanging slightly
weighted, without commendation
halting at zero, passing through an outer wall
so simply absorbed that it has to be bolted
We are by nature emotionally incontinent
with no need for a new shtick—
We've tried all we can think of—and opened up
as if to sing
in the dawn around the close of a church

I'm leaving this place of inclusion
whose bodies were meant for
the earth—with a pleased recognition
of family connection—oneself appears smaller
from behind—a place
comes and goes—a next one has to come again
to celebrate and dance in new forms
leaping over stiles under the sandstone

UNDER THE WHAT

She's off, clamoring
quietly while I'm tuned to
"supposed to," differing lights and sounds
organized with a center
that tries, hard, to make something out
Make it less or something
more demanding. What is everything when settled
against the dust motes in the back of a truck
leading to hills
A dog barks, the third time shriller
less self-assured. Sky bids au revoir as
another life comes in, with prospects
on how these frames and films appear
sometimes without warning—
Who is who and ready to receive
and act the part; demand, or invite others
and what about what's
floating down the river?
A break in the action
even just to let a moment of this
slap and dash accounting have its say

SOAR KESTREL, EYEING FUR

Motion saw and light on wire
Portion of intelligence
Creek-viewed bump of plump
something. Oar out
Anyway you've come this far
That face
blazing, glazed cranium
pearl, two-knit bone and one
in fire. Then dream on
You can't unravel yet to, say
quarrel with her work when she won't
work in portions clear, or opulent—Middle Park
Red truck years ago— crab leg
ranch and wind; line poles. Time was big
fueled from fire in a
fear knot unprovoked
to the south. They have to play there
Rails go by
What kind of look next looks like home
These places people I have known
in shadows you her face did fall on

THUS WE ARE THIS

Was real for you that love was
everybody
disagreeing—reality being real
It's been a long night. So many
came together and then "What's left?"
The question was
How to get home when the love
in your heart is still where it
was trying to get out of—Gone now along
What used to know and not be known
directly—an old show of
hurt—it doesn't matter
what. How is he with babes?
See how she runs
What comes
The last mark fired
and karma released, or reissued—
A new ear grows into it
Beneath written
"comes and goes" but in which
generation of whom?
Your story's moving on horizon scales

MICHAEL STEWART

FROM *DREAMS RECORDED*

JANUARY TO APRIL 2012

14 February. I have watched her nibble on odd things—hair, paint chips, finger nails, paper, ice, needles, string, cigarette butts, burnt matches, chalk, coal, small stones—I met her at the bookstore, she had stolen a page from a book and was eating it. She is slowly making a moon—right now she says it is the size of a dime, a pearl, a bean, a walnut, a child's fist—in her womb. And everyday her pull is stronger.

17 February. I'm vagabonding the country with a friend from high school. We've done something reprehensible in Minnesota and so we're bouncing from one storage area—where we've squirreled a lifetime of stash—to another. We make it to Waco, someone hot on our heels, when I realize I've left my nails (square rather than round, a handful of the wicked things) in a hotel in Utah and I've got to go back, capture be damned.

4 March. They have asked me to embalm my father and despite my protest I am here in the basement (my old room, posters and black light still on the walls) with a bread knife. His belly is distended; I pull from him: a handful of sea shells, a split garden hose, a wooden owl the size of a baseball, a child's shoe, a bowling ball, keys, a music box that still works when I try it.

18 March. A girl, who has a living beetle as the jewel of her necklace, whispers to me. I cannot understand her. She tries again and I hear only the final words: *...the causes of chastity.*

1 April. The girl from Geneva removes, one-by-one, feathers from her mouth while we sit in the hotel bed and watch a silent film on the television.

At first she reads the intertitles for me, but slowly, somehow, I begin to understand them. The movie, which started midway, played as follows: we see the hero—dashing—trapped in the walls of a stately place. Intertitle: *Our hero has gone from one tight spot to another!* He shimmies; a cut away reveals that he is between a debutante's bedroom and her father's study. The father is pacing, a gun held to his chest. The debutante—lovely, dark eyed, dressed in a transparent slip—is sleeping. Our hero stops and pushes his ear to the wall. Intertitle: *What is this he hears! The dreaming girl talks in her sleep!* As he listens, he smiles, he swoons. He cannot help himself, he whispers to her. She stirs but doesn't wake, the father investigates the sound. His sweet nothings influence her dream, which she continues to narrate. It is a kind of conversation. She says, *I'd bet you'd be sweet to eat, my pretty* and starts to chew on her pillow. The father smiles cruelly and aims his gun at the wall. The hero says, *I'll lick your pretty, my sweet*. He fires, she startles awake, looks around and begins to remove with a perplexed look one-by-one feathers from her mouth while the wall behind her bleeds.

4 April. We are watching a speck move across the face of the moon. My father explains, *That's Michael Collins. If we had strong enough binoculars you could see the other two still up there, bored and hungry. Been stuck there since sixty-nine; God knows what keeps them alive.* He says, *You can still hear them sometimes.* He turns on the radio, it hisses static at us. *Well, sometimes.* What do they say? *Not much.* We wait, the moon is moving across the sky. I push the binoculars closer until they hurt the ridge of my eyes. The radio stutters to life. They say, *We are the moon men, fuck you!*

14 April. After the wedding I find myself back at the wedding, friends from high school and strangers mixed together. (The girls with a perfected slouch and sway, like lazy S's. In short, floral dresses.) Everyone is polite. There is a beautiful girl in a little dress; the men are circling her like hungry moths. Under every chair there is a party favor: a copy trumpet, a handful of keys. Under my chair is a black notebook with the names of every woman I've slept with written in slated, meticulous handwriting. The names are a kind of rosary. There are also stray facts: her cat's name is Soap, she has a bruise shaped like a bird on her hip. And mostly meaningless questions in the margins. When I wake up I still have one stuck in my mouth, like a stray feather: *Where have the summer dresses of my youth gone?*

REBECCA BROWN

TRANSGRESSIVE MEDITATION

I used to sit with a Buddhist sangha. They were very good people and I loved learning about Buddhist thought and Compassion and the quiet and the spareness of the room—black cushions and everyone wearing black and sitting facing in then sitting facing out and in the middle, walking meditation. I loved the chanting.

After our sit on Friday mornings (6:30 AM), we'd stick around and have coffee and talk. Mostly we talked politics, and mostly we all agreed. Mostly we were liberal Democrats and pro-gay and anti-war and pro-worker and all the right things. Mostly we were white. Nobody there was Asian. We'd all come to Buddhism as adults and all for good, true reasons. But as much as I wanted it to work for me, after a while I realized something was not quite right about it for me. At first it was just little things—like I had to drive to get there and I'd get there all agitated about the drive and the using of gas and all that (I rarely drive). But really it was a more amorphous thing. I felt somehow that temperamentally—*culturally*—I guess, I didn't fit. As much as I wanted to absorb that whole "no-self" thing, and the "empty your mind" thing, I just couldn't. My mind was always buzzing (I realize most peoples' minds buzz, but mine really is kinda nuts). Compassion made sense to me; but what I missed was human passion. I missed the Self.

I'm all about the personal, about the drama of struggle and death and passion and needing redemption. I'm all about the West and Western Europe; those are my roots, my DNA. I know genealogy isn't destiny, but sometimes I kinda feel like for me it sorta is.

So I found myself heading back toward the Church.

In my world—liberal, educated, artsy, middle class, and white—it's fine if not actually cool to be a Buddhist. (Despite the affectionate sneer of one of my Asian-American writer pals: "Watch out for white Buddhists...") It's less fine to be Christian or Catholic. The fundamentalist wings of Christianity and Catholicism are full of scary people who oppose same-sex marriage, reproductive choice, and females in general. These people include Rick Santorum, Newt Gingrich, Archbishop Dolan, Liberty University, and the late but not lamented Jerry Falwell. Those wings make a lot of noise publicly and a whole lot of misery for people like me (female, gay, pro-choice, left-leaning). So how can I even bear to go near Christianity or Catholicism?

It feels like it wasn't a choice. It feels like it pulled me. Or, rather, it pulled me back.

Though I have a billion problems with the administrative structure, power differentials, anti-feminist crap, etc., of the Catholic church, I love the central story of it: i.e. that there can be redemption and renewal after death and pain; that mercy is better than hatred; that people need to be loved. I also love the Progressive wing of it—Catholic Worker soup kitchens and shelters and anti-nuke clergy and pro-gray priests and nuns on the bus.

I also love, inside church buildings, the quiet.

Which is how I found myself in a "Sacred Silence" group in my parish. We do something similar to what we did when I sat and meditated with the Buddhist sangha. But instead of describing the intent or goal of sitting with language of the "emptying of self" or "no-self," in this Catholic "contemplative prayer," the idea is to be quiet enough to be aware of Divine love (whatever that means...).

Going to sit silently in my church with a group of others has become a really, really important part of my week. We don't socialize as a group or talk politics (though I suspect this particular group of Catholics and non-Catholics I sit with vote pretty much the same way...), we just sit quietly.

In the summer we can see the light change around us as it comes through the stained glass windows in different angles. In the winter we trudge there and home again after in the dark. Sometimes, when the church is being used for something else, we'll sit in a little chapel or in the library of the Parish Center. Sometimes I sit on a pew or a chair, sometimes I sit on the floor in the posture I used to sit in with the Buddhists.

In some ways I've felt "transgressive"—but not in cool ways, other ways—about the fact that, given my lefty, liberal, artsy, Buddhist-sympathetic world, I have returned to Christianity. I feel as if, in some way, I've transgressed against a self I tried to be that didn't work. Now I'm trying to get over feeling the need to explain why I meditate with Catholics. Maybe sometimes it's transgressive to just go home.

ROBERT SNYDERMAN

SASKATCHEWAN

They will know
me from the left corner of my mouth
wanting
work
in Canada,
the
absent welder
in a group
of hands bigger than my face
and a face

Saskatchewan

Above Ontario
why the

"JESUS" / YESHUA

The park in Denver's
center smells
doused in alcohol
the Mexican child
preaches names
of G-d
like the names
of poisonous
wildflowers
and the shadows
of the black-green
park benches
and the gun
strapped to the hip
of a police man, this
protector giving
warnings to
all of us.
All of us crippled the same way.
All of us mute thieves in the orchard.

ORAL TRADITION

the white
principal
in the
many small wounds
along my fingers
Goliath
fell to
his
knees.
I rested against
the
Bronx in his chest
he didn't build it alone
talking to the students
asking them about their families
tell you. told you
my
back will bend then break.
You can't own what you can teach.

“I DONT BELIEVE IN WAR”

we have bad teachers
in Evans, Colorado
and Texas
we feed them
blood in the churches
water turned
to blood
and pay them
nothing and
raise our
children
to become
their
adopted
children.

NORTH CANADA

20,000 students for years kneel before the small fire in the small room
is my generation running or sleeping?
I think we have to   believe in something.
To know the word   we   with difference
(not in difference, not indifference)
is a belief.

BARBARA HENNING

MY ANIMAL EYEBALL

Greg is in the pool with the boys, throwing them into the water, one after the other. "Me, me!" They laugh and sink to the bottom then swim to the top.

I'm pushing the boys in a double Cadillac stroller. They look up at the trees as I call out—maple, sycamore, oak, elm.

I slide open the back door and they run into the yard, their little boy bodies naked in Hurricane Irene. Round and round in circles they run, the wind exploding the trees. They leap and yelp, twigs with bunches of leaves scatter over the yard and streets. Here and there an overturned tree. In my hand, I hold a leaf with a meticulous design, veins branching into the flat green, either a Balm of Gilead or a poplar. On the news, a fifty-year old man rescues a child in a body of water with fallen wires. The man is electrocuted, and the child is in the hospital with bad burns.

When I take Jean's garbage out to the curb, I see a young man two doors down walking back and forth in front of his house with a swaddled infant. Every window in the house is lit up. I ask Jean if they have a new baby. Hard to tell, she says. She usually keeps her doors locked and the blinds closed so there's no temptation on the nautical mile.

Luke sits at complete attention through the highs and lows, the loud and noisy *Lion King*. When it's loud, he holds his fingers in his ears. Mostly, he is mesmerized, sitting straight up, steadily popping popcorn into his mouth. I keep whispering to him about what is going on. When the mother lion cries about her lost husband and son, I am teary. He gasps now and then, but no tears. Like a Shakespeare play, the brother steals the crown away from the son. Then back home, his little brother Lolo is awake, and we three go to the park. Lolo stands on a stump in the park, saying to himself, as children race around him—"I'm tall, I'm tall." Then he sees a little girl, his size and he says to himself in a whisper, "She's tiny."

On my cell phone, I call up *West Side Story,* Richard Beymer's body, and Jimmy Bryant singing "Maria, I'll never stop saying Maria." I'm singing along and the boys start dancing and singing with me. Luke sings with a high five-year-old voice, "I once kissed a girl named Maria." Then they both whisper, "Maria, Maria, Maria."

Luke wants to get a pillow from upstairs. He tells me, "Stand up here on the stairs, Gramma." Then he races into the dark room and back with the pillow.

The weather is warm and spring-like. As I pull the boys back home in the wagon, the earth rolls over, facing away from the light, and we are left with its absence.

Every time I angle across Houston, I think of Ted Berrigan's daughter, Kate, hit by a motorcycle and killed. Today I ask Bobbie if she had three or four children because she has only mentioned three and somewhere I read that she had four. She starts weeping. Leslie, she was killed when she was eight-years old. I'm so sorry, I say to Bobbie. Later Lewis tells me that Leslie was playing in a sand bank and there was an avalanche. Children are not supposed to die like that.

I wake up this morning in the middle of a dream. Linnee is a little girl again and she's running around the room, crying. She stops in front of me and says, "I want someone to comfort me like Dad did." I take her in my lap and hold her. What a deep ache it is to lose each other over the death divide.

I cut out animals from old *National Geographic* magazines, making a booklet with a silly story inside. Tapirs, bongos, gorillas, and red ants. Life is full of animals. While writing this sentence in my notebook, my eyelids start to drop and then my animal eyeballs roll back into wherever the mind goes when it goes.

THE DISTANCE BETWEEN US

I put Anna Kavan's *Ice* back on the shelf. Nightmarish violence toward a childlike woman who is accustomed to being abused.

Read Andrew Levy's *Nothing is in Here* and "Cracking Up." Words of absence, boredom and the inessential, the impossible un-particular particulars in their dis-particularity. The views of the subject lean toward: "I'll tell you later."

Reading "Civil Disobedience" while watching a Youtube of NYC police pepper spray a young woman protesting at Zuccotti Park.

I have profound thoughts during the day, but by midnight, I forget what they are.

Reading Yang Jiyang's book on her life down under, during the Chinese re-education. Humans have the possibility and sometimes the habit of being systematically cruel.

Over three hundred years ago, when Olaudah was a small child, he was snatched from his family. Then he was sold to slavers. I turn over on my other side and listen to the refrigerator hum.

Emerson talks about going deeper than "thinking" into "knowing."

I open a book, read a few lines, walk to the desk, turn the sound up on the tv. An ordinary man slightly overweight, unshaven, mid-forties or so—he has his arms around a woman with a gun in her hand. "It's over," he says. "Your mother is gone, put the gun down, Laura." She's weeping and holding the gun between them. Suddenly it goes off and they both slide down to the floor. She's dead and he's bleeding, but alive. Deeply affected by this woman who executes men who have abused women, he now needs to get some sleep. During commercials, I read an article about manifest destiny and divine rights and the way we invent rights to justify whatever our desire might be. Today a two-year old was shot in the face and my throat is sore.

TO BE IN THE FILM

A sign on a tree in front of my apartment building—Walking through here means you agree to be in the film.

Last night a guy woke me up at 4 am, singing right under my window with a mike and an amp.

Met Mook in the park to shoot him at a chess table, the camera with its viewfinder aimed at catching something and making it still.

The air cleaner is buzzing. "You are walking too fucking fast," someone down below screams.

Laughter and voices echo upward. "I stuck it right in her pussy." That's it. I shut the window and turn on the air.

Outside it's cold and chilly. When I open the window, it feels like a rush of illness.

I water and stroke the aloe plant on the window ledge and I can tell that she likes it.

Many of the trees are losing their leaves and I'm starting to forget sex. That's what happens after a while. Then that wave splashes all over you again and you tremble with lack of leg against leg.

Hands in pockets, hats pulled down over ears, a group of Chinese women wait for groceries, hanging plastic shopping bags along the rails. The line extends from Avenue A to the park entrance. Later left behind, a few white plastic bags fill with wind and then collapse.

On Christmas night after twenty-four hours in cars and suburban houses, I drift off to sleep. All is quiet except for a few drinkers who revel down below.

Someone is yelling outside. Someone is honking. I hear a television in another apartment. Just because I was wounded doesn't mean I must cocoon for so long.

Turn on the tv and watch an old *Law & Order*. Mr. Big was just a squirt cop back then. The Republicans are destroying each other with their phony attacks. We remain hopeful.

MG ROBERTS

BACKLOOP BACK

This is the sound of chromosomes multiplying haphazardly, looped and out of sequence.

a. What is a sound?

b. What is a haphazard sequence?

This is a range of memory: looped information serving as identification for objects it labels.

c. This is naming.

This entire chain encompasses patterns to be read into memory. Reading memory is, entirely red, made of patterned sight called vision. I called and called.

d. This is able.

I heard the sound of the making after it arrived and it was news meant to be burned. This is the sound of a chromosome dropping from the sky: notice its amplification. Underneath, packages of tightly looped thread-like structures divide into a long chain.

Through motion make heard sound, red entered our mouths and said I object to this arrangement! And all motions were repetitive, looped like sound, or like the way loops of muscle fibers remember.

FERRIED

Past the calamity
Of incubation
At a stretch of blue
On all sides of diagnosis
Water swells

Water is a glass of
Soured milk where
Red ant bites blanket
Bite the itch of
A scene to begin.

HR HEGNAUER

FROM *SIR*

Dear Sir,

When do I get to be *and* now?

All I want to do is say, *I and you* in the way where *and* is a verb, like I *do* this. I *love* you. I *and* you. Do you understand what I am saying now?

How do I account for the space between paragraphs? Sir, this question haunts me. Please, make it stop. I want the spaces to stop being so fond of the gaps. I am writing to you from here: from the place where language doesn't sound like a sentence anymore because it's forgotten its breath.

Andrea says that *their lungs helped them to arrive*. Sir, why won't my lungs help me like this? I move them, I do—like this and sometimes a little bit more like this, but they forget.

Dear Sir,

What does a shadow look like when you're dead? Is a penumbra the same sort of thing as the two words *Mark Twain*—the place where the safe water begins, but in a shadowy form, not in a watery form? Sir, I am making us a language! Come and meet me here. I am extending to you these middle waters and these middle shadows. This is a held place. Believe me. I have been here for a while now, and I still want to be *and* now.

Dear Sir,

I am trying on narrations, and this is what it feels like: a pocket of red string. Who is the evacuated narrator? This is you, isn't it, Sir? Please, tell me this is you.

Look, it's like this: I can either see the humans right now, or I can see the words, so the humans are going to get a bit blurry. I want the words. That's all that I want. This is a want that has all together forgotten what to do with wanting.

Dear Sir,

I am afraid to say, *I love you*—a collection of simple sounds. I know this is the softest room in the body, but the navigation is so —. This is what it means to swim in a vivisection, and I like swimming; I do, but I need the tide to be more clear. By this I mean my thoughts: I need them to just stay a little longer. Please Sir, just stay a little bit longer now. Come with me! It's time to walk.

Please, help me to hallucinate a clear tide.

Dear Sir,

Were you here again last night? I'm a little bit confused. I heard you in the echoes when you said, *Watch out! This is your body*. But then I couldn't find you, and I looked; I really did.

But then I took that bit of blow from that boy who told me his name was Peter Valentine, and I wanted to believe him.

Sir, I am evacuating all of my bodies.

Dear Sir,

Last night I watched Dan walk out the window of his high-rise apartment. I followed him. *Someone else* watched us do this.

Then I awoke to Danielle calling me, and when I answered she said, *Thank god you're alive!*

Later, Rachel asked if anyone else dreamt about the apocalypse last night. Yes. Sir, *If living had to be about the body, who made it so?*

Dear Sir,

What time is it? A damp translation. A row boat. *A sack of a baby.*

This is gone though, Sir. *Of ever imagining that.*

Don't you get it now, Sir?! *Or ever having wanted that.*

Listen to me, Sir. I know what I'm talking about! *Or known it. From someone.*

Sir, are you *someone* now? No, you're just a ghost. A spook. A haunt and a specter. You're a shadow now, Sir, and you can't even visit these colors anymore!

What is it like? Is it like skittering? Please, take my hand. Tell me it is.

CHRIS MARTIN

FREEDOM

So there
is this God, right?
Demure
as fuck. Like
a sort of subtraction
from air. Less
than breathing. A breeze
that makes way.
A wind that when you
move moves
in the other direction.
Or maybe it kind of blows
a little of its own
to help yours float.
Not touching, just
a whisper, silent. It's
less than everything
so everything can be
anything, this God.
Our devotional minus.
Like it all
began when God grew
weary of nothing's
balance and sucked back
from zero to make things
possible. Removal's

invention of the is. Like God
was standing there and then simply
retreated
a bit and since
then God is forever
stepping back, swallowing the tiny
dots of language
that might otherwise surface as
declaration, sweeping leg
after leg out
of the way, a grand
untouching tango
where we can't not
lead, like that line
of Sartre's I'm always
repeating, *What is*
not possible is not

to choose, an entire plane
of existence stuck
in the on
position and only
God there to offer subtraction.
God is the not
and we're the not not.
God's not detonates
us
into not notting
forever and we can either
not not or more
simply we can hazard.

FAITH

To read *oppositional*
posture is a lab where dominion
invents its vaccines. To stop
reading
the page. To see this
headline skewered across the leafless trees.
Their cotton buried under snow.
To breathe light
like anything deeper might
portend conspiracy
where tiny bubbled molecules of dominion mass
flood the body and harden
into a dispersed seed
nest
for cold
reason and its obliterating bloom.
To half-gulp one's
coffee, then, for it too, now,
has cooled through the dominion
of time into a soft, brown, belated
hole
where mincing entropy
can tooth all
of life's fabric into vague pills that wait
for Sarlacc-like digestion
in a forgotten pocket.
To pull one out and *squish.*
To think vaccine
into the room, miracle
stretched to cover what debasement
plagues the injurious heart
of "life"

where we all function like vaccines
until we don't. To don't. To finally wrest
some stuttered no
from the overstuffed clutch
of compliance, if only
to kill it, to rip through the blank
of zero's

stitching and turn
the whole of its negative
form inside-out. To forge
an affirmation
there in the clutter of its gut, amid
tiny planets of absence
like a lone and ever-full moon
and see how "to" itself
puts affirmation at risk and return
to Dana's words worried
at thought, how through thought
distance is also dominion, like in Schuyler's old
proposal, where "to have thought"
to do something
might be equal to its actual
doing, but that can't be right, right?
Not to write a poem, but
to move through pain
of all this clobbered thinking
and see word
mean as much as wood and poem
tree. I know it won't.
Not yet. But maybe then, that other
now
we don't
know
will ever come. The one
I have to believe
believes it will.

SOCIETY

Existence like a blank
check, paying
day to the breakneck flower
sun fluffs. I mean
we all, *eventually,* get up.
Grow
palatial to grow so
very little. All
shirts today.
Tomorrow pants.
A hand almost
too alive in its veined wriggle, its
desire
to fill a pocket, I mean
stuff everything
and sweat into folds.
I take everything
off on
purpose. Stomach
goodbye
navel waves. Gonna shake
shake shake shake
shake your face. I love anything
that jitters overstuffed
with the tropical duties of gratitude.
I love all woke
with, yes, definitely, *too* alive.
Like the dancing chicken that ends
Stroszek—they told Herzog
it was a stupid idea. Terrible stupidity.
Heroic stupidity. I want
is an endless supply

of quarters like weather, so
Herzog *was* wrong about the chicken: the sky
is falling is the dance. Goodbye
luffing hello.

PORTFOLIO 1

DEBBIE CARLOS

MT SI

IAN RUMMELL

5

1

4

9(2)

ANNA JOY SPRINGER

IDENTITY AS ENCOUNTER:

I AS THOU IN DISCONTINUOUS MEMOIR

My work of the last ten years emerges in part from a tradition of lesbian confessional writing. I performed with Sister Spit's Rambling Roadshow hosted by Michelle Tea and Sini Anderson in the late nineties, where the topic of most stories was the self-representation of mostly third-wave dyke feminists in their twenties, mostly white, often from the working classes, with a post-punk sensibility. In this subgenre of memoir, the character representing the author is often a fabulous heroine, even when she is a fucked up, blacked out, sexually damaged anti-heroine. She has adventures, and she experiences grave upheavals and threats. She rails against injustice, and she's right to shake her fist. She does a wild-eyed glittery pogo to the manic beat of drug-addled calamity, lying girlfriends, confrontations with her perpetrator, and S/M gone wrong. She's often hilarious. In the late nineties, in cities across the US, I witnessed Sister Spit audiences cackle and moan, riveted by these true tales. They found themselves, super-fun, super-gutsy versions of themselves, represented, finally.

Although my literary tastes pulled me in the direction of writing that complicated notions of transgressive identity, I was even more excited by unanticipated story-specific poetics and staging as a medium for enacting these complications of lesbian experience. Try as I might, I failed to write an accessible version of myself as a swashbuckling, hope-inspiring mess of a heroine, and my stories would always slump into a sort of allegorical suicide of over-wrought despair. I was unable to engage the Sister Spit audiences with the restless, para-logical looping inquiries I wrote, stories that for me signified selfhood, even sisterhood. And it's ten years later and I'm still writing books that could be called "confessional." Why do I continue to mine this genre? Am I yet another woman looking for love in all the wrong places, asking my imagined readers to tend to my wounded wounded heart? If I were a real writer, especially a really investigative curious writer, shouldn't I write about subjects outside of my personal experience? Shouldn't I stop embarrassing myself and everyone else with my inaccessibly written but still overly personal pleas for mommy?

Irene Gammel writes in the 1999 anthology, *Confessional Politics: Women's Sexual Self-Representations in Life Writing and Popular Media*, "In [this subgenre], the authenticating female body behind the speaking and writing voice somehow endows the woman's voice with *an implicit realism and truth value*, ... The sixties feminist slogan, 'the personal is political' has further increased this trend, *although the association of confession with sin, shame, and voyeurism has made many feminists weary of the practice*" (1, italics mine).

How to hear these stories without being crushed or, alternately, embarrassed by a sense of trans-personal victimization? How to hear them without feeling non-consensually thrust into a sort of tragic exhibitionism? We call cliché those cultural products reproduced so often they seem redundant. Women's confessional writing reinscribes ad absurdum women's personal experience, experience that is so often shared to the point of shameful banality. And on top of feeling that topics of abuse and liberation are banal is humiliating, is that feeling of "Why don't I care? I should care. Whether the writing is boring or not, I should care."

I say my own work is partly rooted in this 90's lesbian incarnation of "the confessional" and, saying that, I cringe. It is somehow too PMS, too cat-box messy and simultaneously too 50's wifey-controlled, an embarrassingly decorative pity party with sagging balloons. All the usual terms come to mind: narcissistic, self-congratulatory, masturbatory, lazy, porous, pathetic, blobby. Which brings to mind Beauvoir's description of feminine sexuality: "Feminine sex desire is the soft throbbing of a mollusk...woman lies in wait like the carnivorous plant, the bog, in which insects and children are swallowed up" (386). If I didn't know this idea of feminine sex desire was meant to be insulting, I would read it as titillatingly perverse. So, driven by both natural devilishness and a desire for justice, I perform a possibly perverse reactionary response, mainly because women's confessionalism is maligned in the same terms used to malign women. As a feminist, made politically conscious through the crass and operatic aesthetics of punk rock, I am suspicious of opinions that stink of misogyny. I practice saying the word with a threatening sort of *defiance: "Con-Fession."*

But I also come from a lineage of feminist experimentalist and contemporary criti-fictional and fabulist writers, and my work probably reflects this aesthetic inheritance more obviously than that of the confessional. To further confound this gesture of self-positioning, I am a Buddhist, and philosophical-spiritual texts inform my writing to a great degree as well, especially my notion of self-as-character. I yearn for encounters with people and objects that allow me to sense our inter-being, what Martin Buber in *I and Thou* privileges as the more gratifying of the two pairs of "basic words," I-Thou and I-It, by which he means the terms describing human existence as primarily relational. He says, "The basic words are not single words but word pairs. One basic word is the word pair I-You....the I of the basic word I-You is different from that in the basic word I-It."

As a writer, I work in the artistry of the discursive, but nearly every day, I also engage truth-seeking in *nondiscursive* meditation practice. Training this way, I see my mind and its thoughts as something "other" to my self. My daily understanding of myself is: myself as a series of roles, myself as a character in interaction in systems. When I see myself as the roles I've assigned myself, I create an I-It relationship with myself, but it is through this relationship that I am able to enter dialogue, and the possibility of dialogue allows me a way in to conceiving of myself in relation to this "other." And relation is what I want. I agree with Buber's notion that "Relation is reciprocity. My Thou acts on me as I act on it... Inscrutably involved, we live in the currents of universal reciprocity" (68). My relationship with others, ones I conceive of as myself and ones I experience as outside myself, allows me to see myself and my environment as a relational system, rather than an autonomous, willful agent. It allows me to feel involved in the world I create and am created by through interaction.

Both in meditation and in writing, I am interested in creating the space and focus required to meet myself as I-Thou, with the Thou being the character-other I create of myself. It is a practice I can do without the presence of another person, without even the presence of a tree to contemplate, but my hope is that it is not a solipsistic exercise. My hope is that in this dialogical exchange, I am training myself to transform my relationship with all other beings too. To experience the basic word, I-Thou, in all my daily encounters. To be in dialogue with the non-self objects comprising my systems of interaction. So although my work features versions of myself as character, although the work "confesses" my should-be secrets, it is far from a solipsistic pursuit, or at least that is my true intention.

My book, *The Vicious Red Relic, Love,* is an illustrated, multi-genre punk novel. It looks like a regular postmodern novel in its changing genre and format, multiplicity of literary voice, and dizzying aesthetic experience. At the same time, the book expands literary approaches of feminist experimental writers using collage techniques to dramatize central themes of contingency and relationality in identity-formation and contextualized variability of power and language. So, it's a postmodern feminist spiritual confessional novel with pictures.

It's also a love story. Its narrator and compiler of texts, Nina, looks back through old college notebooks, journals, and literary and scholarly texts to try to reconstruct the course and demise of her first lesbian relationship with [Gil]. [Gil], who was HIV-positive and showing signs of AIDS-related illness, committed suicide on September 13, ten years before the 9/11 national emergency in 2001. As an investigation of grief as a true phenomenon and the search for a working-notion of "self" at the millennium in an over-developed country, Nina begins compiling a scrapbook of her time with [Gil] in the context of their queer punk subculture in early-nineties San Francisco. The book presents and revisits a variety of texts that intertwine to develop the narrative basis of [Gil] and Nina's relationship. A non-sentient literary object "Blinky" becomes a comfort both to Nina and to [Gil] in retrospect, and is one of the main relics of "love," an expression of desire both created and undermined by the text itself.

In *VRRL*, my main character is Nina, and Nina is a literary manifestation of me. Nina is not I, but a representation, or a series of representations.

At the same time, in the stories I tell myself about myself in my daily life as a living being, I am a representation of me too. I narrativize myself as a character to be read, decoded, and internalized by myself and other readers, and this is at the cocktail party, this isn't on the page. I project myself to myself "the patient devoted girlfriend," "the wise mentor," "the abject griever," or the "freak among the together ones." I enact these roles, as best as I'm able, and as I negotiate the series of overlapping readings and misreadings, I image manage and try to gauge my efficacy, reading your cues about how you're reading mine. Like a person, a character is also a moving object in a field of discursive objects, in exchange. For readers, a character represents a potential "I" and an "other" at the same time.

If a reader has access to the character's thoughts or intentions, the reader shares intimacy with the character, more intimacy, possibly, than with another person or with themselves. When a character's thoughts are revealed, readers are offered a form of communion with the character. As writers, how different is this kind of communion from the one where we look back at our old writings, marks we made that externalized and ordered objects of the mind, how different is this communion with a written character than with the character we find ourselves to have been in the past? That past person, the one who described herself to herself in her gold-lock diary no longer exists. But she doesn't NOT exist either. She is not dead, but she is not alive. She has become a coded object, a set of material and discursive remains. She is a memory. As an older person now, your mind contains elements of her mind. Your cells are different, but the pattern of what they contain is the same or remarkably similar.

Nina, my "me" character in the novel, is multiple and discontinuous. She's more than *one* set of concepts coalescing in a description of her physical and psychological features, habits, circumstances, and desires. At different points in the novel, I've written her in both third and first person, as either Nina or "I." But when in the first person, she's variably "I back then in history" or "I right now in history" or "I, trans-historical, in literary space."

Nina, in her various character forms, is revealed through short story-like chapters and diary entries, but also in illustrated ephemera-like course notes, drawings, ads, and brochures. Some of these images are scanned, as-is, from my own college notebooks, and I have reassembled some into visual poems and other pictures. Typed diary entries from 1991 and from 2001 work in tension to create a projection of the character's trajectory and to reveal the basis for Nina's excavation of her old notes. In researching her old traces, she is trying to piece together a relationship with her first girlfriend, who killed herself, but also to intervene and undo a mistake she made. She could not change her actions when she was twenty, but she wants to try to now. The older Nina feels a deep sense of regret that [Gil] died lonely and alone.

That is to say, *I* feel a deep sense of regret. I wish there is some way I could have offered [Gil] a more abiding love. I am discontinuous with the role of witness I have given myself. Because of this discontinuity I am beside myself, my self's other. Who was that girl I was when I was 20 and so checked out? Who was that me who did not believe that people create and are created by their interactions with one another? Are she and I here together now, or did she die too? Did I leave her unwitnessed without a companion as I left my first girlfriend?

To reconcile all these grounds for grieving, I compile a novel, which, because it is a novel, sucks all these events, revelations, and wishes into discursive space—something like memory, and something like fantasy. Discursive space is not temporally historical because all events happen in language, in the present. I can rearrange the order of causes, and I can change or erase effects. I can construct multiple contradictory outcomes that don't cancel each other out. This is story, not event. I'm under no delusion that the real dead will come back to real life or that mistakes can be undone. But within this flattened or congealed literary space, I can, via my characters, go back and offer my first girlfriend a friend, a witness to her suffering, the witness I could not be. And in my encounter with myself as 20-year old Nina, I can offer her a witness too. I can try, in literary space, in which all causes and effects share the same temporal range and all characters are fictional, to create an encounter between my discontinuous fictional selves, including myself as I write. And I code my reader as skeptical witness to this intention, this experiment in love and grief.

Thich Nhat Hanh describes the "self," which he puts in quotes to signify both its slipperiness and hold as a concept, as comprised of five elements:

form, feelings, perceptions, mental formations, and consciousness. The last three of these five aggregates testify to the relationality of "selfhood"—perceptions, mental formations, and consciousness require a separate object to perceive, form a thought pattern about, or be conscious of. In this configuration, we are relational beings, our being coalescing in and contingent upon relation.

"In its essence Being-with-others is not a spatial but an *ontological* relation," writes Buddhist existentialist Stephen Batchelor in *Alone with Others*. "That is to say our coexistence with others is not merely accidental [. . . .] but is fundamentally constitutive of the very way we are" (72).

If meditation is an encounter of self-in-relation, self-interbeing, it is an ineffable encounter. And it seems to me that the very definition of "spiritual" hinges on this sense of the fullness of inarticulable knowing. At the same time, I experience this longing or even compulsion to translate this experience in language—to *lay it out* as a map and prompt for a concrete mental formation. To crave both dissolution in a sparkly field of volitional interbeing and the externalization of that state via mental formation equals portioned, rationed, separate, to be a slimemold with the spirit of a poet, there's the rub of desire. Martin Buber describes this impulse as the inevitable outcome of an experience of I-Thou encounters, writing, "This however is the sublime melancholy of our lot that every Thou must become an It in our world" (68). And I long for the It, the he or she, the other, to become re-transformed into a Thou—this longing is a sort of loneliness, with a bruised but open-hearted edge to it. It is not a statement in a dialogue, nor a resolution in monologue, but a question—an unstoppable and tender reaching outward.

In her book, *Don't Let Me Be Lonely*, Claudia Rankine writes, "Then all life is a form of waiting, but it is the waiting of loneliness. One waits to recognize the other, to see the other as one sees the self." She quotes Levinas, who writes in "The Transcendence of Words," "The subject who speaks is situated in relation to the other. This privilege of the other ceases to be incomprehensible once we admit that the first fact of existence is neither being in itself nor being for itself but being for the other; in other words, that human existence is a creature. By offering a word, the subject putting himself forward lays himself open and, in a sense, prays" (120).

Buber states, "The longing for relation is primary, the cupped hand into which the being that confronts us nestles; and the relation to that, which is a wordless anticipation of saying Thou, comes second...In the beginning is the relation—as the category of being, as readiness, as a form that reaches out to be filled, as a model of the soul; the *a priori* of relation; *the innate Thou*"(68).

And the Sufi mystical poet-philosopher, Rumi, wrote:

> This longing you express
> is the return message.
> The grief you cry out from
> draws you toward union.
> Your pure sadness
> that wants help
> is the secret cup.
> Listen to the moan of a dog for its master.
> That whining is the connection.

Hear me roar or hear me whine? As I am writing the memoir novel, I am also its reader. As readers write, so writers read. Like language, genre, and other fiction prompts, literary character is a set of triggers that might alter the reader-writer's story of herself as a character-in-relation. This reader-writer character endures continual destruction of a solid stable self by being in relation, by being altered.

Is there any chance of freedom from the distorting mirror of shameful confessional mollusk-like womanish narcissism? If the literary character can prompt a reader-writer to confront and engage her own uncertain self, the literary character may also offer a pedagogical model for engaging with other discontinuous selves, other *people* living as both character-others and potential Thous. That is to say, it may be possible through writing and reading to learn to encounter one other spiritually, witnessing this profound and shared loneliness.

Batchelor, Stephen. *Alone With Others: An Existential Approach to Buddhism.* NY: Grove Press, 1983. Print.

Buber, Martin. *I And Thou.* Trans. Walter Kaufmann. NY: Charles Scribner's Sons, 1970. Print.

de Beauvoir, Simone. *The Second Sex.* Trans. H.M. Parchley. NY: Vintage Books Edition, 1989. 386. Print.

Gammel, Irene. *Confessional Politics: Women's Sexual Self-Representations in Life Writing and Popular Media.* Ed Irene Gammel. Carbondale and Edwardsville: Southern Illinois UP, 1999. 1. Print.

Levinas, Emmanuel. "The Transcendence of Words." *The Levinas Reader.* Ed. Sean Hand. Oxford: Blackwell, 1989. 144-149. Print.

Rankine, Claudia. *Don't Let Me Be Lonely: An American Lyric.* Saint Paul: Graywolf Press, 2004. Print.

Rumi, Jalal al-Din. *Rumi: The Book of Love: Poems of Ecstasy and Longing.* Trans. Coleman Banks. NY: Harper Collins, 2003. Print.

Springer, Anna Joy. *The Vicious Red Relic, Love: A Fabulist Memoir.* Seattle: Jaded Ibis Press, 2011. Print.

ANNA AVERY

THE DIARY OF WATER

Drink the air. It is silver. It is water.
It is cool and reflective in convex lungs.
Inhale the possibility. Exhale the sentence:

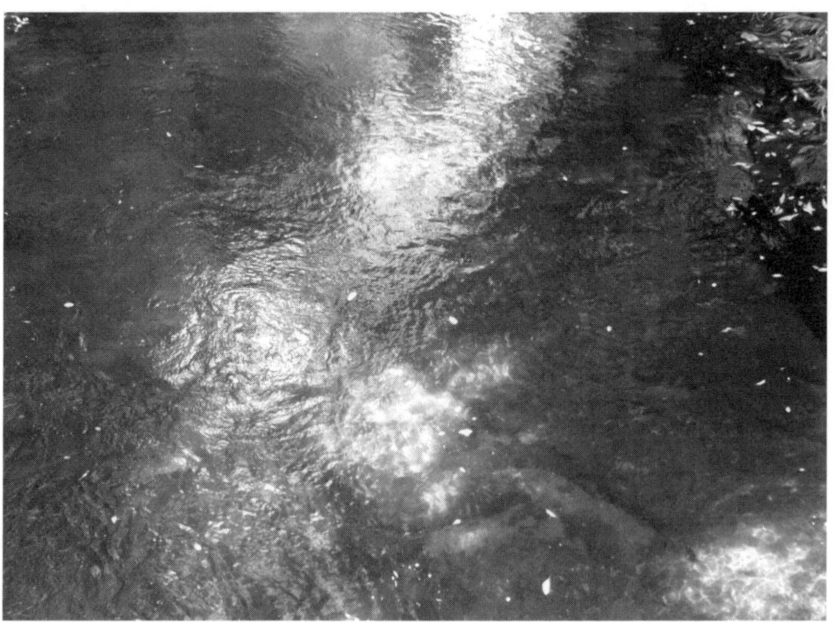

My name was given to me by two people who did not know me.
They only knew that my body was made by their bodies. All, bodies of water.

The body is water.

A roving sea of

Intricate

Intensities

Secrets repeat.

Shhhhhhhhhhh.

Water rushes in blue roulettes, forming cursive in the waves.

Water is not blue. It is not a mirror to the sky. It is a mirror of its own. A mirror of movement, twirling and reflecting its own soft metallic image back at itself.

Swirling eddies white foam white noise water digs into itself beneath tan and pink granite rocks curve. Water is intelligent, aware of itself. Waterfall underneath movement foam, ripples agile skin, gold pools underneath the water is warm. Shadow shallow and permeable soft metallic membrane. Triangular waves irregular scales layering. Rocks hold space for water to flow. Turbulent crossing over millions of large and small pebbles and boulders. These rocks form a line, then a curve, gouge delicately into the land. Green around the perimeter of the water, reflects into the water, green and grey. The water pushes and breaks itself in a continuous flow. Smells of green and washing, the water struggles up walls of rocks and creates a current through motion. In gentle abruptness, the curve of the line opens up to expansiveness, a pool of stillness and imagined silence, a place for sunlight to grow, drench in the water, a meadow of water, a young man takes refuge and bathes himself in the holy retrieval.

Articulation of Water:

Shhhhhhhhhhhhhhhhhhhhhhhhhhhhhhhhhh
Hhhhhhhhhhhhhhhhhhhhhhhhhhhhhhhhhhh
Hhhhhhhhhhhhhhhhhhhhhhhhhhhhhhhhhhh
Sshsssshhhhhhhhhhhhhhhhhhhhhhhhhhhhhh
Hhhhhhhhhhhhhhsssssssshhhhhhhhhhhhhhh

Soft dirt
Souls of feet
Melted earth
Soft earth
Walk on the breast of the earth
Walk on its flaccid extravagance

copper pennies
of sunlight
mix into metallic
mirror of the
current

Underwater:

A face. Plunged forward.
Mouth opens into sky.
Blue on blue. Blue is
Soft and choking. A gentle
Hand. A gentle grip. Clutching.
Around. The throat. Little pearl
Fingers. Lace around the throat.
Prodding arteries.
Nipping for a pulse. Quiet.
Quiet. No room for speech.
Under water. The volume is
Too heavy, too anchored by
Echo.

Drowning, I can see you clearer.

Fine powder, blue black moisture, blue veil. What endures? Gnawed and thawed flesh. What is it to be formless? To be dead? Once you are dead, the narrative is no longer your own. You are confined to the memories of others. Your narrative is their memory–changing and fading. Fluid.

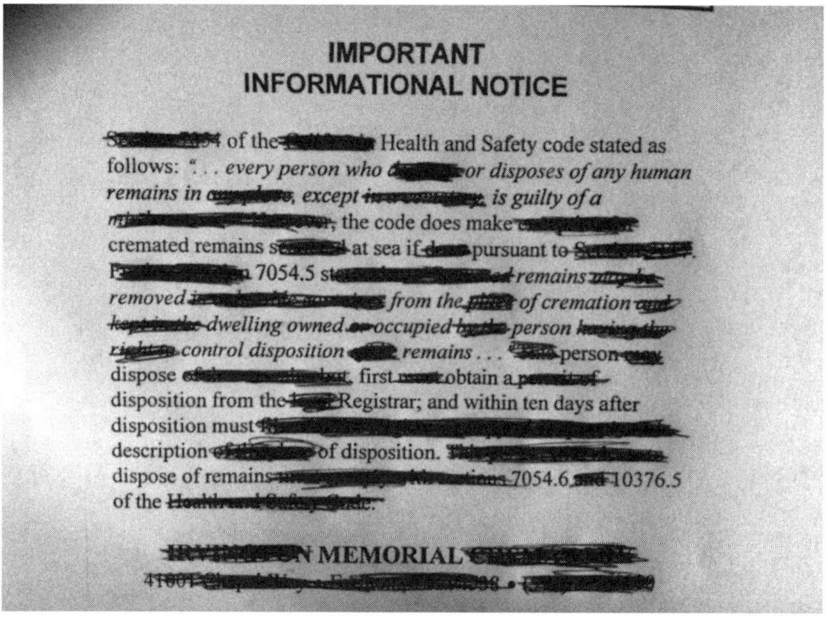

IMPORTANT
INFORMATIONAL NOTICE

of the Health and Safety code stated as follows: "... *every person who or disposes of any human remains in , except is guilty of a* , the code does make cremated remains at sea if pursuant to 7054.5 *remains removed from the of cremation dwelling owned occupied person control disposition remains ...* person dispose , first obtain a disposition from the Registrar; and within ten days after disposition must description of disposition. dispose of remains 7054.6 10376.5 of the

MEMORIAL

Visions from the dead. Remembrance under the window sun peaks into the second story hardwood floor studio apartment. The sun warms the bed, the body of a young woman hunched in a curl, draped in gold curtains, against a grey brick wall. A mobile of deer bones circle above her, whispering purple lullabies. Calligraphy weeps, holds my heart with its giggling fist in a gesture to protect. What has been hurt, what feels pain Love songs crawl up sweet spine boughs. Two women together on one bed. Drenched hours gleam pink noises. Satin magenta circle of her solitude. Circular sounds imprint sobs, create a fullness, languishes in spacious corners. Tender noise. Tender noise.

Sea. Ocean dark, swallowing the picture of a memory dissipates into sepia foam constructed of bubbles and air. Delicate. Transparent air. Sea foam, womb contains an invisible Venus, I do not see her, I feel her spreading and glittering nakedness. The sea is blue and black and full of salt and brine. How do we know more about space than the ocean? Expansive in its darkness. Expansive in its depth. The ocean holds it secrets in this form:

Dark dark dark dark dark dark dark dark dark
Dark dark dark dark dark dark dark dark dark
Dark dark dark dark dark dark dark dark dark

Trying to describe the thing disrobes it of its essence. Hold it in your mouth for two minutes. Swallow. Drink. Stillness, pause, rest...

Aroma and taste travel more slowly than sound and sight. Touch is the slowest sense. The black is rough and tender in its roughness. Sentimental and collecting. Sediment and grit and slowly building and eroding.

Molecules do not stand still in bleeding cities. Articulate the space between sounds. No such thing as silence, only noise. The nervous system chatters, *He's dead, he's dead*. Prenatal noise. The vow of the vowel and a copper refusal. The spider web fog weaves its way between buildings and cars. Olympia's sidewalk holds my feet, pours the liberation mead between concrete cracks, a gamelan prayer in the overcast afternoon. A slight drizzle rings dark blood, viscous sweat plum wine. Bronze shouts from green leaves. Walking by the Puget Sound up the hill to the west side, the water is thick and pungent.

At the bottom of (my) spine (something) peaks in pain a small hand pulls out a pin needle connecting vertebras to vertebras silver fulcrum slowly seeps out a silver sap at the top of the head. A pain. What pain? An ache in the arm pinprick pain at the top of the head spreads dissonance. People resonate the pain they feel; people slither in between each other in the streets. Do not look each other in the eye. Feel the electricity between bodies. Feel the static between bodies. Feel the static between stations. Feel the static between stationary bodies. You and I feel that we are nothing.

Walking to the water, up 4th street from downtown, up the slope of the hill to the open cavern of water. The Puget Sound is a holding cell.

Tender asphalt, the black surface of the water. What lies hidden under its dark submergence? How lovely the water will feel! How it will cleanse me from this black sticky haunting in my stomach. I reach into my stomach and smell the water. It smells black and gently charred. The sea gulls flap their wings in sympathy, crying.

Filling up time's womb. The womb is ripe, whole, and fresh. Do not pick her, She will choose you. Transmission from the mouth to the other words are realized between you and I in silver touch. Well dressed in our own narratives until the body is realized. Neon blue and pink lights stream up the legs through the feet. The dream and real time know no serpentine. All run in cycles. A bell rings:

It keeps moving backwards and forwards as I'm standing still. Stillness is an illusion as the past pushes the body back. Stomach drops. Future rushes the body forward. Stomach drops. A roller coaster pendulum swing back... *I remember when I you were alive...* swing forward. *one day I will get over you...* stand still in the place where you are. Right now. Feel the sweetness of your present placement:

ERIK ANDERSON

FROM *ESTRANGER*

It is now late summer, 2011, and I am trying once again to order these notes into some semblance of legibility. It has been a long, unproductive season, and I have been avoiding a confrontation with the heap of words that have not, as yet, coalesced. As always, I take heart from Perec, who writes that his books are following a path, are marking out a space, tracing a tentative itinerary, describing point by point the stages of a search the why of which he can't tell, only the how. I believe, he says, that I discover—I prove—the direction I am moving in by moving. Elsewhere he writes of the importance of throwing oneself out into the void, of trusting in life (despite the dangers) and launching oneself into a future without shape. It's an optimistic act, he tells us, not to know where we're heading and to head there anyway; to do so helps us be fully who (and where) we are. We find out where we're going as we go there. It may be that I have, up until now, lacked the necessary optimism, or it may be that this whole time I have been going precisely nowhere.

Early this morning I woke from a dream in which my father gave me his copy of the *Chuang Tzu*, the eponymous text by the Chinese philosopher from the 4th century BCE. I read it years ago, but since then a few remarkable passages have rattled around in my memory. In one, Chuang Tzu dreams he is a butterfly only to wake up to discover that he is recognizably a man. So real was the dream of flitting from flower to flower, however, that he cannot determine with any certainty whether he was a man dreaming of being a butterfly or whether he is now a butterfly dreaming of being a man. My own dream was no doubt a distortion of the time Dad gave me, when I was still a teenager, a copy of Lao Tzu's famous book, except in the dream his *Chuang Tzu* was marked up with marginal notes in my own handwriting. Is this text dreaming me? I wonder. It is only through writing that I become myself, Werner Herzog says, but this bringing into being is also a bringing into banality, and the I that appears on the page may only be real to the extent that it has become a commonplace. Not a butterfly, but a man sitting in a dark basement, quite early in the morning, as the day gathers up above him. At the same time, how *strange* this man appears, so little does he resemble the butterflies of my dreams. I almost want to call him an abstraction, this figure bent over the computer, but that would be even *stranger*: an abstract actualization. Such, alas, is the position of the subject: foreign at the moment it becomes concrete.

In fact, Dad did send me a book not long ago, but it was a book on writing and teaching that arrived one Monday morning in early February. It was an unexpected present, and I read it off and on first during a flight to Cincinnati, and then on the following connection to D.C. Somewhere over Pennsylvania, I read this classroom exchange, in which the teacher, Roger Rosenblatt, follows up on his assertion that an essay requires digressions, depends on them for total effect.

> I ask if they recall the scene in *The Catcher in the Rye* where Holden attends a speech class. The teacher tells the kids to yell, "Digression! Digression!" whenever a student speaker wanders from his main topic. "What's Salinger saying here?"
>
> "That digressions are the only interesting parts," says George. In the novel he is working on, the hero's name is Holden.
>
> "But you can't just digress and digress," says Ana. "You'll lose the thread. You'll fly off into space."
>
> "Also like the blues," says Kristie. "You can go away from the tune for just so long, but no longer. Otherwise you'll forget the tune. So will the listener. So will the reader." My thumbs go up again.

In the book, *Unless it Moves the Human Heart*, Rosenblatt shows himself to be a good teacher, full of fatherly advice. He knows what he believes is good writing and champions it. He's a charming curmudgeon, whose crankiness is clearly a persona embodied for effect. I read the book dutifully, delighted that Dad thought to buy it for me, even if I disagreed with some of what Rosenblatt said. When I failed to finish it on the airplane, I toted it around with me that evening as I rode the Metro to meet an old friend at a restaurant near DuPont Circle—one of his favorites, he told me over the phone. Perhaps it's my inborn resistance to advice, but as I stepped onto the endless escalator at the station, I found myself wanting to write an essay that only grows stranger, that digresses even from its digressions. A text that flies off into space, that loses its thread over and over because its point is not a thread but a life—and the mind that lives through it.

I was in D.C. for a conference, but I was equally there to see Oliver, a friend I had made in my early 20's when we were both waiting tables for a living and avoiding the messy business of what to do with our lives. I had liked him immediately. Strange non sequiturs sprang from his lips, as though he were always two or three steps ahead of the conversation, and yet the sorority sisters who worked at the restaurant found him charming, more charming than me anyway. What he knew he had learned from observing plants, animals, and the systems through which they interacted. I admired this rootedness in him, and when I left Ann Arbor for graduate school, I missed it. He followed suit not long after and began a peculiar program of research, which, as he explained that evening, had raised the hackles of many people in his department. At issue, he said, was not his science itself, but what had been called, pejoratively, his philosophizing. His mentor had been quite supportive, but elsewhere he had encountered fierce resistance to his project, which, he said, was invested in bringing science out of the academic journals. You see, he continued, our problem in the sciences is not so different from yours. Specialization is a kind of perpetual cocoon, and when the other larvae see you breaking out they get defensive.

Our number was called and, after walking downstairs to pick up our food at the counter where we had ordered it, we sat down at a table in the cramped upstairs dining room. The building struck me as an odd place for a restaurant; from the outside, it looked like it had once housed an embassy, and in fact I had spotted several in the neighborhood. Inside, however, the colors were warm, and the walls displayed the work of a local photographer—cityscapes, mostly, with the occasional portrait thrown in. As we ate our bowls of udon, Oliver asked about my own work, and I told him, in a shorthand way, about Herzog and my notion of estrangement. He wondered whether I remembered the scene in another Herzog film, *Encounters at the End of the World*, in which he interviews a biologist named Sam Bowser. Vaguely, I said. Bowser's team is engaged in deep-sea dives beneath the ice sheet, he explained, where they are cataloging species that live more or less sealed off from the world above. In the film, Bowser discusses several varieties of foraminifera or forams—small protists that live along the seabed. The forams have a system of pseudopodia or "false feet" they use to eat and to move—long, tubular strands that extend from the cell wall—but the creatures are most remarkable for the tiny shells they produce, called *tests*. As they gather material from their surroundings to build them, they select certain particles and reject other, less suitable ones. It's almost art, Bowser says. Herzog then asks—with great care, he says—whether Bowser would call them intelligent. Bowser cites in response the case of the mystic, microscopist, and scholar Edward Heron-Allen.

See, it's funny you mention Herzog, Oliver said, because this other film has everything to do with my work. In 1915, he continued between bites of his meal, when Heron-Allen, as the newly elected president of the Royal Microscopical Society, suggested that forams possessed faculties akin to intelligence, the members of that august body were less than pleased. They were appalled. Under pressure from his peers, Heron-Allen later backed away from his claim, which had proposed two criteria for intelligence. First: the forams selected certain materials and rejected others for the construction of their tests. Second: they applied these materials in highly sophisticated ways. Where forams and other protists would eventually fail to meet the definitions of intelligence that developed in the twentieth century would be in their failure to remember and to learn. At some point during the long and scattered history of memory in protozoa, Oliver told me, experiments comparable to the mouse in the maze were conducted. The protists couldn't remember where the cheese was. The point, he said, is that once these experiments were done, it pounded a coffin nail in the debate. Memory may be no less tricky a criterion, Oliver told me, but choice is problematic because all living things (and even some non-living ones like a virus or an antibody) select one thing or another. But the real trouble with saying forams are intelligent, as Heron-Allen discovered, is that it introduces certain anthropomorphic suggestions that arise out of the word *intelligence* itself. In other words, Oliver said, intelligence carries too much human baggage; we can't apply it to animals without thinking of ourselves.

The bigger question, he said, is how do we divide human life from non-human life and what does this division entail? Certain members of my department tell me that it's a better topic for a sociologist, but for my part I want to see the forams within a continuum that ranges from the smallest expressions of life to the largest. And more importantly: if human activity (everything from books to buildings) is basically no different than the agglutinating matter in the forams' shells—that is to say, a product of selection and application—at what point does that activity cease to produce a test? And would any such division be an arbitrary one? Order subordinates, he said. Definitions divide. To say one species is not another may be a straightforward distinction, but to say how—or, more problematically, why—the human species has "risen above" the rest of creation is thornier territory.

By then we had finished our meals and were leaning back in our chairs. Oliver had an early meeting in the morning, but said he had time for a beer or two if I wanted to walk down the block. We took the side streets in the general direction of the station from which, in a couple of hours, I would ride the Metro back to my hotel by the airport. We crossed over Connecticut Avenue, and walked down a few steps into a cavernous underground bar lined entirely in wood. Oliver brought a round over to a small table along the back wall, and though we had spoken of lighter things as we walked—mutual friends, the drizzle—once situated in the bar we returned to our earlier conversation. The Italian philosopher Giorgio Agamben, he said, believes that the boundaries we establish between man and animal are slightly more arbitrary than they appear at first glance. He doesn't go so far as to suggest some mystical connection between all forms of life, however. He's more concerned about how these boundaries reflect, on one hand, political realities and, on the other, how they reverberate in the psychological make-up of human beings.

We must learn, Agamben writes, said Oliver, to think of man as what results from the incongruity of these two elements (the human and the animal), and investigate not the metaphysical mystery of conjunction, but rather the practical and political mystery of separation. For what is man if he is always the place—and, at the same time, the result—of ceaseless divisions and caesurae? It is more urgent to work on these divisions, to ask in what way—within man—has man been separated from non-man, the animal from the human, than it is to take positions on the great issues, on so-called human rights and values. It's not that these things are unimportant, Oliver said, but they are screens for a categorical humanity and animality, each of which arises out of their opposition to one another. Before we can address our shitty pay, shabby health care, lousy schools, and the ongoing ecological holocaust—before we can "fix" a Haiti or Kinshasa—we must first establish the degree to which our meatpackers have become extensions of the cattle that cycle through feedlots, slaughterhouses, and supermarkets. We must recognize the degree to which Haitians and Congolese, among others, have been allowed to wallow in structures that define but don't ameliorate their conditions, and we must acknowledge the degree to which our own urban poor are quickly following their lead. And then, he said, there are the animals we have come to think of, on the other side of their cage walls, as a subordination of the human world. We would be foolish to think that the technological management of life on the planet is possible, let alone desirable. To think that a species can be "saved" or the warming of the planet "stopped" may be hubris on an imposing scale, but it may also miss the point. There is no mastery. We are not creation's saviors. And so, Oliver chuckled, all that remains is the complete rethinking of the categories of life.

I went to order another round, and when I returned Oliver was still smiling. So, he asked, are you going to use this in your book on strangeness? He drank deeply. I told him I wasn't sure what animal intelligence had to do with it. I had to be kidding, he said. Hadn't I ever said my son was acting liking an animal? Oliver said when his own son, Lucas, was born he couldn't get over it. I kept telling Molly how this was animal life, how what Lucas was living was the closest to an animal he would probably ever get. She wasn't convinced, but then, he said, we started reading to him. In children's books animals speak in such a childlike way. I've always found this humiliating, not so much for the children, but for the animals. I bristle at *Carl's Birthday*, for instance, when Carl, a Rottweiler, and Madeleine, a toddler, unwrap presents together and add sugar to the punchbowl. They manage to fill up a helium balloon in the shape of a reindeer. And don't even get me started on *Are You My Mother?* Do you know it? A mother bird feels her egg beginning to jump and realizes she has nothing for it to eat. After she leaves to find food, the bird hatches and begins to look for her. It asks a kitten, a hen, a cow, and a dog whether each is its mother; the ones that answer say no. At that point, the bird comes across a large excavator; naturally, the baby bird asks the machine if it is the bird's mother. The excavator, in which no driver is visible, picks up the bird and drops it back in its nest just in time for the mother to arrive with a tasty worm. I'm still figuring out, he said, what to make of the fact that while everything else is rendered in dull colors, shades of brown mostly, the backhoe is bright red—and of the fact that, unlike the talking animals, the machine can only snort—but industry, I read, will save you.

I told him that it might be because of interpretations like his that many children's books—books like *Goodnight, Moon* and *Brown Bear, Brown Bear, What Do You See?*—eschew plot altogether. They use formulaic structures instead, in which each subsequent page is a different version of the preceding one: even though you can't get some of these books out of your head, I told him, there's less room for hokey theories. Once you figure out the formula, you can relax: nothing's going to happen that hasn't already happened. A brown bear sees a red bird, a red bird sees a yellow duck, who might then ask a turtle, a frog, or a fish whether they've seen a stray duckling. As much as I was tempted to read this as a lesson about narrative itself, Oliver was more interested in the way these books make the natural world conform to the human one. Of course the animals speak, he said. Of course they have consciousness. Because if we didn't recognize ourselves in them—and the natural world of which they are a part—we would be like outcasts or bastards in their midst, instead of vice versa. Whether or not the authors intend to, he said, they encourage a cuddly version of the animal world, one that teaches children to be friends with nature even as they're conditioned (sometimes subtly, sometimes not) to become its masters. People talk about "raising" their children, but they mean something like raising them above their animal impulses. The sooner a child sees an animal as human, the sooner he might recognize that an animal is not human—that the human is above the animal. So we're back to that, I said. We're back to that, he said.

But the fact is, he continued, it takes very little to turn us into animals again. Did I ever tell you, he asked, suddenly serious, about our intruder? He hadn't, I said, and in the dim light of the bar Oliver's face turned pale for a moment. He began to tell me how, the previous summer, there had been a break-in at their apartment. He and Molly had been asleep when she awoke to a noise coming from the kitchen. She shook him and whispered that someone was in the house. He told her she was imagining things and turned over in bed, but she was insistent. You're the man, go see what's happening, she said. Oliver thought about that for a moment. He stood and walked out into the hall. In a sleepy haze, he could vaguely make out a figure moving towards him and telling him firmly but quietly to sit the fuck down. He had a gun, Oliver said, or at least what, in the dark hallway, looked liked one. The man peered into the bedroom and waved Molly out of it. He pushed her down next to Oliver. The two of them, he told me, were shaking. Don't hurt us, Molly kept saying. Don't hurt our son. She started quietly crying, and the man, who had not likely counted on us waking up but was nonetheless prepared for it, led us, Oliver said, into the living room. He quickly duct-taped our hands, ankles, and mouths. I can tell you that in those moments—particularly at first, when it wasn't clear what would happen—whatever made us human receded into the distance. We were back in the primordial soup our ancient ancestors had evolved lungs and legs to crawl out of, where it was all fight or flight, kill or be killed. The intruder, Oliver went on, worked efficiently, avoiding Lucas's room altogether. On the kitchen table, he stacked our laptops and phones and some of Molly's jewelry—he had found the diamond earrings her mother had given her and which she was too ashamed to wear. In the dim light trickling from the other rooms, we could make out his silhouette but not his face. Before long, he turned off the lights in the bedroom and office and went into the kitchen, where we saw the refrigerator open and shut several times. We heard the rattling of plates, then he emerged carrying a small backpack, presumably with our things in it, and a sandwich. The backpack he placed by the door, but he carried the sandwich over to the living room. He sat on a chair opposite the couch where, to the extent it was possible, Molly and I had regained our composure.

It was an odd hour to be leaving the neighborhood with a lot of stolen property, the man explained. His voice was well-modulated, an educated voice. He would wait until five, he said. There would be a few more people about then, and he would stand out less. Oliver looked at the clock. It was four. I have no interest in hurting you, the man said. This—he lifted up the revolver as though it were the heaviest object in the world and returned it to his lap—is just a tool, no different than a hammer at the end of the day. He took a few bites out of his sandwich. He complimented us, Oliver said, on the arrangement of our apartment. Very Zen, he called it. After he finished eating, the three of us sat in silence. The sweat on Oliver's face was loosening the duct tape on his mouth, but he really couldn't imagine calling for help. Who would hear him? The man heaved a large sigh out into the room and said that he could see they were good people. He felt he owed them an explanation. This was the shape of it, he said. There was nothing for him to do. He had resisted it, but only recently had realized how foolish his resistance had been. If I'm smart, he told us, Oliver said, I can do this for a few years and disappear—Brazil, maybe, or Thailand. And if I get caught, well, I have no illusions about any of this. My justification is my defense, not that the courts will care. He spoke in a general way about his upbringing, which was, Oliver told me, very middle class. The intruder claimed to have done well in school, and even to have graduated college with a degree in Theater. Oliver didn't know what, if any of it, to believe, but the man was convincing enough. He never apologized, Oliver said, but he was struck by something apologetic in the man's tone. Before long, it was nearly five and the man carried his dirty dish into the kitchen, where they could hear him placing it in the sink. When he left not long after, Oliver hopped into the kitchen to get the scissors with which he and Molly then took turns cutting each other loose.

They recounted the story to police later that morning, but the officers weren't surprised. There were ongoing investigations, they said, and yes, there had been other robberies. The whole experience had thrown Molly totally off, and she had started to see a therapist. After a few months, she came home one day from a session and told Oliver that if the intruder was ever caught they couldn't press charges. That really shocked me, he said. Here she had been so terrified and angry, and then to come home having transformed that into something generous. She had realized, she told him, that there was no way to make the intruder leave her mind now that he had entered it. He was there, and she had to make a home for him. Things were replaceable, she said, but the man's life was not. In fact Oliver had gone out and bought a new computer the very day of the robbery, and he had thought at the time how strange it was that what had been so difficult for the intruder to acquire had, after a phonecall to his insurance agent, been immediately resupplied for him. That capitalism keeps happy even its semi-successful agents—Molly was a lawyer, after all—came as no surprise to Oliver. More startling was the way the theft had been treated by everyone involved (the police, the neighbors, the insurance agent) as an animal act. Even more troubling was the question Oliver had refused to answer to nearly everybody who asked it, excepting the police: the question of the man's race. There had been something insinuated in the question that he couldn't quite stomach. The animal experience, in any case, had been Oliver and Molly's, not the intruder's. He had been perfectly rational, genial even, whereas Oliver and Molly, according to him, had been overtaken by evolutionary impulses they had rarely experienced and poorly understood. Oliver had been so taken by the poignancy of it that he had, for a moment, misunderstood the neighbor who in hearing the story had whispered, *animals*. He had thought the neighbor was talking about him. We were both a little drunk by then, Oliver and I, and it was getting late. I speculated about how the case of the intruder compared to the case of the stranger. I would think, Oliver said, that they are almost inseparable.

As he walked me back to the Metro, his descriptions of his research, now that he had several drinks in him, sounded less like the work of a serious scientist and more like the musings of a slightly cracked mystic. When I said as much he laughed. To him, the best science walked a thin line between metaphor and fact, and he had long ago left behind any affinity for researchers who didn't ask questions that were larger than the scope of their studies. I should read Lynn Margulis, he said. If he had it all to do over again, he would have gone to study with her in Massachusetts. She has the remarkable distinction of terrifying most people she comes in contact with, Oliver told me, especially men, although she often writes with her son, Dorian Sagan, who is also the son, as you might expect, of the late Carl Sagan. The science is solid, but she's always asking herself, what's the significance? We scientists often can't see further than the microscopes in front of us. Or mass spectrometers, I suggested. He laughed again, but by then we were back at the huge escalator that descended into the depths below Connecticut Avenue. We wished each other luck and parted ways, and it was only when I was comfortably in my seat on the train that I realized I was still carrying *Unless it Moves the Human Heart* and that, earlier in the evening, I had meant to ask Oliver what biological basis there might be for an essay that flies off into space.

SARAH HEADY

THE HIMALAYA

What I did not feel in those two minutes:
a sparkling peak, a parachute jump
idle at the edge of a fishless sea,

the pain of old men studying hard
for a supermarket job test,
their gill feathers falling
ember-like, industry emblems,

a ferry departure, the forgone
civic space of the waiting room
bright as ex-kerosene Dreamland,

arcing orchards with spun
sugar harvests bundled in plastic
sheaths to shut kids up,

ancient clay dogs on the Hudson's
shore reborn and reborn,
aborted clown young

early laughed at, gone
as the flintspark of Man's
First Comedic Moment (in a cave
somewhere in France: present-day
site of the Moulin Rouge).

INJUNCTION INVOKING CALLIOPE

Someday the sun will become
a giant traffic circle
and we will all be complete:

scuffed bocce balls swept under
shag rugs, personal parking
spots staked out with bedsheet
ladders and plastic rakes.

When we are gathered
around the coffee table after the long
awkward meal, the spine of the book

lying there will be uncracked.
The broken keys of a calliope
will be our new best jewels.

ANGEL DOMINGUEZ

[A PAIR OF TRIPTYCHS]

I want to unravel inside of you, turn to synapse, make a garden there—wish I were with you now in the after of it all—where have all our good ones gone?

Swallowed by hunger for erosion—replete with color and scent of concrete, rough cloth; unwashed, stiff with time:

I wrote myself into a cavity with capacity for reception. A precipitation of palpitation—really the rhythm of everyone with lungs really, it's the bursting of every heart making memories—losing all the dead parts in juniper berries, lost in the liquid of transient poetry the way we all breathe and die, can be dead and breathe with infinite lungs—the paper of the mind makes for meandering rivers of tongue, even the dead ones sing:

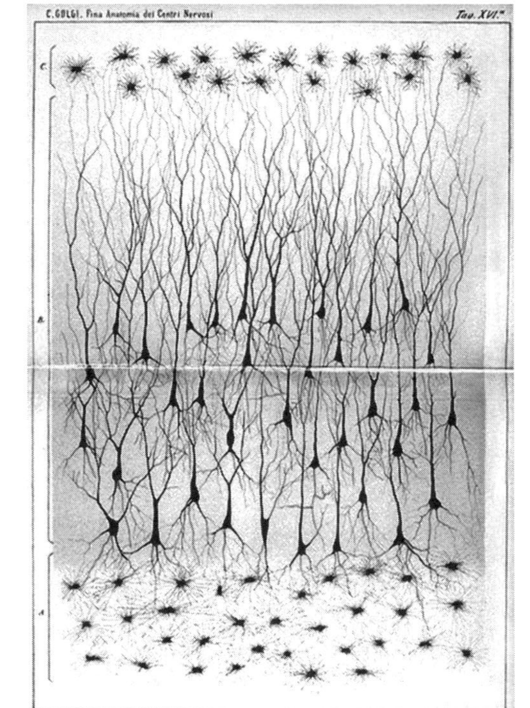

Memory is nonlinear—forgetting anamnesis is not a place, but a process, picking iron flakes from aluminum always seeking articulate reflection, a soft photon amnesia: a blue rust stuck in back of throat, coming up dry as dull—brown is only a deep red. Changing what we inherit from our past lives. Time is but a callous—transparent frayed by memory I drew you using blood—it curdled into brown amoeba and we never spoke again aside from when, you fly into my dreams as a small blue coyote, lost in a forest of axons and dendrites—I told you I hadn't forgotten about the way we once were, burnt chemicals; animals losing their empathy, becoming a history of nonrecollection; that which was, is no longer, yet here we are now

Opening chambers to change out
the strange capillaries, having
grown blue lips, oxygenless
malignancy, shifting angles of
light—connected by photons
inheriting the hunger for sun and
long light waves
Digging in vocal vestibules for some
semiotic sense of next; the bends,
how it hurts to blurt out blues of
Outside made inside—solid lines,
liminal. Non-linear triptych modes
of thinking, moving mouths to form

Mitosis, starts the motions of breathing—I am
outside of you, I want you inside of me. Here
where I am nothing but the outwards facing
skeleton made flesh by mirrors and other eyes

Refractions of time tubes—a long gone list we
can't approach from the outside, always inside
forming dwelling—I stay nomadic, haunting
every ice cavern, alpine & mountain dirigible

Moving forward from fragments we form
vestigial architecture—forgetting makes us
time enough to make or murder—make red:
long form stretching light reaching for anoesis

We inherit that which we forget, finding far off
outlines of ragged lungs, the lonelies we've
collected and kept to disassemble, to scatter a
fragrance of movement: clockwise: lemon eye

Time can move about the face excavating that which is bokeh—barely there glints of bone & hair, those human things bespoke remembering: hippocampus breathing, I wanted to build a body of light—diaphanous heart nectar. The earth spins anti-clockwise, centrifugal are the skies too big for eyes, memory too works this way: mutations unexpected, sudden sharp and made of aging iron: evacuate to hot coffee mornings years from now where you are when that is, still in a state of osmosis—time heavy and sipping. Splitting, we form a rhizome, we chalk into diaspora—peripheral debris, spinning clockwise against the earth seeking recollection through blue conversations, femurs quivering to the closing of eyes in circular fracture, decomposing becomes an arc—turns into arch floating up from the pewter brine. One day we may wake up hylozoic

SERENA CHOPRA

FROM *THIS HUMAN*

MAKEUP, THEY PORTRAYED THEMSELVES WOMEN—

PREMISE 1:

Beauty is an architecture perceived without the application of a particular sensory organ.

Rather, it is the negative space between objects that define beauty in terms of proportion and it is the object itself, in interrupting that space, that is either complete or not.

And then light, expelling a cosmic charm, allows beauty to migrate the field of shadow symmetry.[1]

PREMISE 2:

Organisms are the organs of the natural world.

There is light in each organ, carried as potential, as a momentum unlike gravity, ungiven to that power.

---

1 Steinberg, Charles Side. "The Aesthetic Theory of St. Thomas Aquinas." *The Philosophical Review*, 50:5. Duke University Press, 1941. Web.

But when we clutter the organs with electric spasm, the natural light, the true moon and day, are hushed.

Even kindling is superficial; the fire needs something to sink its teeth into.

PREMISE 3:

Beauty is reason.

This means that one can know beauty beyond its pleasure to the senses.

The body, in its entirety, is a sensory organ
detecting and interpreting beauty.

PREMISE 4:

For this, language pains itself into poetry.

The human mind works towards reason, is content when it is complete and full
of similes, the formula positioning beauty
is a formula like any other, but the variables are infinite.

Like stars, like stone, like water as bone—

The world was perhaps beautiful before humans, but
being the natural world's organ of reason, humans
have the capability not only to read beauty, but to understand it.

And yet, like other beasts,
humans fall
for attraction.

The fear is: If we are unable to perceive actual beauty, can we still create it?

ARCHITECTURE

The woman sometimes feels like the skeleton of sex.

I was told to examine her but without a light,
I had no apocalypse to compare her. She was a body
and a body and a scent and a skull.

For her anticipation, I brought her trachea and
larynx. I brought her a suicide, domestic
brothel and endoscopic lineation. What
is the pain against her lung? What would she ask
had her mouth been without pronunciation?

Respite clutters her, is dire air, like fog, between beauties; is dire air,
an architecture. Much of what is built is negative,
a space-ridden conjunction—And then we walked through,
or around, which were our homes—ugly, ineffective, anticipation-ridden
from which I brought her many things.

A form is the human; the most perfect form, light
fills space proportionately. Speak it up, the world constantly
like a cellular prison; the river cuts itself
against the firm and still land. A plastic surgery

plunges into the woman and she is spreading her
body despises shadows, a flag has wrapped itself into half mast
and resembles an aching crow.

The petroglyphs resemble nothing, a narrative, they beg for motion
from a flickering flame. The beauty is captured, is the realization of forms
    breathing time.
The petroglyphs suggest this is enough from a body who plunges into time.

A line is enough to map any beast
not a bird—

Double, triple, echo the line to emphasize intention:
Symmetry is repetition against the light; plastic is repetition despite it.

I admire you, human, but I am embarrassed for the body
once made critical by function and utility and now made critical by
 consumerism,
the conniving utility of a transparent entity, something like power, and
 equally without adequate ends.
This environment has made the physical body irrelevant.

The body has become an affect
of the individual who possesses it, who is falsely convinced of its significance
and is sacrificed plastic atop a mound of market.

This looks like the architecture of a modern middle class home.
The architecture of an actual body is more honest.

insert images of architecture

Of all the organs, only eyes are for sight, only ears for hearing, only tongues, etc.

Where in the figure is death?

There, the brutality of living

tamed

Here, to be merely biological—

an egg or corpse

and to lapse between these.

Remember, and

to be a conjunction—

light unravels silence

follows each word

a history

etc., Of all the organisms, only humans are for beauty.

MATTHEW COOPERMAN

SPOOL 34

I take seat
where body bends
remembrance in habits
of who attends
the morning chairs
the morning light
in sinews too
the sweetest tea
inform the shareholders
what is high
and what lows
communicate the addresses
to our cells
a self recurrent
pattern of presents
my commodity flow
to unwrap ease
set table high
with golden light
you particular you
to shine across

§

a figure against
a black background
structure of all
perception is this
reach in things
how they stand
out and about
next to and
within a field
green with clover
our riotous color
a sexual craving
opens the nose
insistently these curves
a mood appears
to dissolve clarity
sniff animal kin
among constancies irregularities
a pre existence
insistent dog time
of our flare
a fleeting swarm
it is summer
love both sight
and shadow's flower
another day enslaves

§

scholia made us
a book sense
different by degrees
separation as policy
is what won't
work the general
from the major
misapprehension our hand
from a claw
declension as if
we're all removed
putting it down
the letter animal
a thing made
historical surety so
poignant we weep
and rage both
worlds ring true
see it clearly
a blue ring
our sweet okeanos
from shining sea
grant me the
next enduring organ
a savage intimacy
we made this

§

stars our destination
a scaffold in
the trees to
climb ourselves misericordia
into and over
the big idea
of cell pull
it's to scale
in our tides
however tracked traced
the apple ladder
of your eyes
what wondrous green
stars stirs stars
in our vanishing

MICHELLE AUERBACH

CAN I DO THIS SPIRITUAL DRAG

"[C]an I do this spiritual drag, collective agony wishful thinking, fearful peek-a-boo actuality about to be read in unapologetic disinterested participation against fantasy without benefit familiarity . . ."

—kari edwards *Bharat Jiva*

"uggghhhhh, i am only halfway through this interview between akilah oliver and kari edwards on queer subjectivity in poetry (queer as in : how to actually make language supple enough address the material realities of LGBTQ people) and i am a little bit high and i hate that they are dead and i hate that passing for me is pretending that chris kraus' i love dick has anything to do with my life and i hate that we are always talking about the abject straight girl's abject love for straight men and i don't think we can talk enough about akilah oliver and kari edwards and why isn't everyone talking about them and where are my queer poet mentors and how many fucking academics get paid for a lecture on halberstam and fucking gagafeminism and how many shits do i give about your boyfriend and how much of my life have i spent trying to identify with gay men and how much of my life have i spent trying to identify with straight women and how much of my life have i spent hating my dykey-ness and how much do i need kari and akilah tonight and why am i thinking about lorca addressing whitman and ginsberg addressing lorca and whitman and where are the other chronologies where is my imagined space of address where can we speak to the other dead queers where are we where are we where they where are they"

—Jane Cope "akilah and kari"

"There was no one I knew with a deeper commitment to looking for something real in the heart of the façade. Maybe she would learn to face the truth, and like the truth she faced? (She was 45 when I first met her, and would be 55 today if she had lived)."

—Kevin Killian "Long Ago Tomorrow"

"[R]elating to or affecting the human spirit or soul as opposed to material or physical things . . ."

—OED definition of spiritual

The Lord Shiva in the Hindu tradition can appear as both male and female, either/or, both/and, all of the above. There are statues of Shiva with one side of his body dressed and adorned as female with an identifiable female anatomy and the other side in male garments with male anatomy. The statues are dynamic, moving, dancing, never still, always in flux and in transition. In the Shaivite tradition, the play of the masculine and the feminine manifests both strong gendered roles and fluid sexuality but always winks at the illusory, cardinal identification with the physical form as essential and dangerous. In the diverse and eclectic history of Hinduism there are myriad ways to approach the problematic physical body in a spiritual world. There are strategies of going in deeper, getting out faster, cooling, heating, moving, stilling, and flagellating. There are moves to engage in dangerous and transformative magic and ways to leave behind individuality in favor of divine connectivity. The body is crucial to the undertaking of spiritual evolution. It is a transitory vehicle for incarnation and engagement or disengagement with the illusory world of the sensate.

At a Naropa Summer Writing Program workshop in which Steven Taylor was discussing the differences (none) between spirituality and poetics, kari edwards' philosophical poetics began to resemble spiritual philosophy. The conversation turned to the previous summer and to edwards' belief that poetry and philosophy want to find a way to break us out of the illusion and give us a glimpse of the divine. This was a sentiment edwards elaborated in conversation with Akilah Oliver "poetry attempts to get to a deeper truth by trying to describe the indescribable." All the poetic tricks and turns and jumps, for edwards, boiled down to conveying a slanted, altered, other view of reality that moves us deeper into our bodies—negating our existence and exploding and exploring and staking out the no space of the subject who will not stay still. In *Bharat Jiva*, edwards writes, "when we mention the people, we do not mean the confessional body of the people, we mean the particularly itinerant bodies in mechanic flux" (3).

The perplexing tension in edwards' work is that the body is there to be transcended at the same time as it is the tool, the vehicle, the necessary and perfect structure with which to take "a joy ride though the absurd" ("Narrative/Identity"). The body, according to edwards in an interview with Lance Phillips, is "what allows me to feel others and the universe. If I want to speak of the possible I have to be in touch with the present present in the body that is my body." The bodily experience is both singular and plural. It is made of distinct singularities that never quite adhere to the rules of the dominant culture yet provide little interstices that both separate and bind. The body, that other to spirit, is necessary to accrue the details of worldliness in order to see how the individual differences manifest as the overarching idea of difference and exclusion—"if beyond the self, is the self beyond essential multiworld universal non-escapable caring" (*Bharat Jiva* 76).

The epigram at the beginning of *Bharat Jiva* is from Patti Smith, "oh to be not anyone, gone / this maze of being skin." Escape from the body and the illusion of this reality as separate and individual appealed to edwards. In fact, edwards followed this branch of Hindu metaphysics all the way to Sri Aurobindo's ashram in India. Central to Aurobindo's teachings is the idea that we are transitional beings in transitional bodies on our way to an involution and evolution of consciousness. We can see this reflected in *Bharat Jiva* when edwards writes, "despite the body / there is a universe / despite the universe / both waves of existence" (104). Aurobindo's dialectic of salvation is based on a poetic undertaking of moving to the depths, finding revelation, and having a complete transformation of experience—bodily, emotive, and intellectual. There is no doubt that this view on the body is also tied to Patti Smith's and intrigued edwards in the quest for no gender.

Yet, the deeply embodied pursuit of the luminous details of the quotidian is at odds: “remembering through bodies / and thoughts of thoughts” (*Bharat Jiva* 106). The entirety of edwards’ poetry is taken up with details of incarnation that bring the reader back into a sexual experience of the body without sex characteristics where fuck stands in for connection and reality is defined as what connects us: “in reality this is it, the end, or maybe a deep understanding that two good fucks is worth one hundred thousand, one hundred thousand dollars and change” (*having been blue for charity* 14).

It is possible to read the classic narrative of the spiritual searcher in edwards’ work: dissatisfied with this plane and with bodily existence, the seeker looks to break the barriers between self and the cosmos and find a sense of belonging to mitigate the yearning and sorrow this realm has to offer to anyone who navigates it in human form. The escape from the body and the escape from illusion are both tropes in the retelling of spiritual awakening. However, instead of this tired but sturdy story, edwards pursues a path of tension of opposites between the body and spirit that holds the both/and instead of the neither/nor. While edwards describes the experience of being in a body in *having been blue for charity* as “I crouch in a body episode” (9), there is also the feel of a “sense of polish and satin” (9) when skin meets skin or mind meets mind that burnishes edwards’ jarring, difficult work.

In other words, the body and the experience of being in a body are complex. The more complex, the better for edwards as the language of the poetry reflects:

> falling in and out of the service of “truth,” to another, for another, in love with “truth.” Repeating you have to believe, you must believe, listen to the mother and the father read books and repeat after me, I can not represent myself, we must represent the not representable whole impossible to represent. (“let us say goodbye”)

This complexity, a fractal iterative form of subjective possibility is the spiritual core of edwards’ work. As Judith Butler writes and edwards uses as an epigram in *Obedience*, “Possibility is not a luxury; it is as crucial as bread." Juxtaposed with grammatical terms and flashes of suburbia and India in edwards' work are definitions of modern life—bank accounts and burger joints and 800 numbers, "call 1-800-complete resignation" (*Bharat Jiva* 67)—with lurid light and a trip through "a field of time, where / there is a choke hold on language" (*Bharat Jiva* 74). These are such glorious descriptions and beloved touches that edwards' deep love and confusion around a body's purpose and necessity is evident. These moments, along with the always more and eternally fecund world of the poetic and spiritual unconscious, illuminate spaces "where the lakes, rivers and oceans are no longer lakes, rivers and oceans but mud covered hunger living in bodies" (*Bharat Jiva* 71).

Another aim of certain Hindu metaphysical technologies is to quell hunger, desire, and other physical needs and demands of embodiment. While edwards mocks conventional religion in America, chalking it up to "cheap prayer to a god subdivision" (*Bharat Jiva* 19), there is the yearning to use yogic traditions to escape the inevitable suffering of being spirit in a body. Lines in *Bharat Jiva* such as "neither delight or aversion / no difference between a thing" (106) echo the *Bhagavad Gita*. Even so, edwards is not a classical yogi, looking to still desire and evade this world in search of transcendence. Rather, in the way Hindu philosophical traditions are always in conversation with each other—questioning, arguing, reflecting, engaging, demanding—edwards turns over experience and looks at it from different angles. In "a narrative of resistance," edwards writes: "shifting and causing interference, not knowing where the 'I' is going, creates the possible out of the impossible" (267). The polyphony of voices and images in edwards' work is a both/and/all strategy to take in human consciousness. The divine is present in the universal spaces around self that form personal connections in the search for where the world, language, our bodies, consciousness, and experience meet and mingle, captivate and repulse. Though edwards uses the first-person singular, the uncomfortable, unreliable "I," it is in the service of a "you" and an "us." As Robin Blaser puts it, this pronoun is "neither first, nor a person, nor singular" (qtd. in Smoler 179). In *having been blue for charity*, edwards writes "just words. You are my consciousness. I am you, sitting there reading of listening, content and embellished" (12). The receptivity and reflectivity of consciousness throughout edwards' work values Aurobindo's tradition, where "the most indispensible thing in every case is receptivity" (Alfassa 257).

In Hindu temporal concerns, receptivity, openness, confusion, and calamity are all parts of the experience of the body. They are universals that, even in dissolving gender and questioning the body as solid or real, draw us together and define the encounter with form and incarnation. However, edwards warns against using "the 'I' as the ultimate achievement, where the endgame is the epiphany of late capitalism," lest we become "a consuming self-controlling anorexic life form on automatic" ("a narrative of resistance" 266). These words invite us to experience the "I" without trying to control or define it. And to taste and enjoy the "I" without trying to morph it when it becomes uncomfortable. The tribulations of moving through this escapade of incarnation are, in Sri Aurobindo's yogic teachings, what creates enough discomfort to open the well-defended shell of ignorance and break the ties with illusion. In other words, to crack a person open and make space for something new: "The task remains as always about reducing suffering" ("a narrative of resistance" 267).

Emmanuel Levinas writes, "The biological, with the notion of inevitability it implies, becomes more than an object of spiritual life. It becomes its heart" (18-19). So, too, with edwards, whereas difficult as the body may be, the body sits itself at the center of experience and then starts causing important trouble. Yet, without a body, there is no heart to crack open and no fragile, precious human existence in which to work towards enlightenment, and edwards knows "it is time to detonate the heart" (*Bharat Jiva* 3). To have the experience of an "I" who does not fit into the either/or gender constructs and to question the version of reality regurgitated in American culture is to feel essential brokenness or failure as sweet, divine, tender and most importantly universal. "[O] ur blood is your blood / our house is your house, listening / for another other's cry for love" (*Bharat Jiva* 75). As the offering of our transitory, temporary, excruciatingly beautiful time here, edwards' work gives the reader an elemental connection of feeling self to feeling self. Subjectivity, like grammar and gender, is part of how a consciousness placed in a body articulates finiteness. Without something at stake, be it self or death, gender or transcendence, or entanglement of feeling, there is no wedge with which to open to each other and to describe what the "I" knows.

The deep "now" and "I" and "us" and "this"-ness of edwards' work is the boon that has carried on, brought people into intimacy and conversation, and fed the need for history and placement of a reflection of self that is skittish, needy, human, and real. If we are to move with edwards' spiritual gesture, it would be towards building a community of vulnerability and lack of stable self that opens us to the possibility of a state in between this and that, now and then, here and there, I and thou, in and out, and singular and plural. This is the gift edwards brings to an awkward, frenetic, unstable search for reality and freedom. The good tidings of incarnation—we are here, this is it, this is reality as I experience it at this fraught moment—can appear as problems to solve or damage to avoid. The pain and the trashy ugliness of our culture and of this illusion of time and space might be enough to drive someone to search out something better, cleaner, bigger, and more comforting. This kind of retreat may wall off the individual into a spiritual materialistic grab for abatement of suffering. Not so with kari edwards, who bravely and gorgeously uses poetic gesticulation to describe and embrace the volatile spaces between illusion and reality. This negative capability, this ability to hold both the arduousness of existence and the possibilities is at last, the deepest move of the spiritual: "Today I watch the cement crumble. Juxtapose love with everything" (*Bharat Jiva* 99).

Alfassa, Mirra. *Collected Works of the Mother*. 7. Pondicherry: SABDA. 1955. Print.

Smoler, Michael. "Unrepentantly Experimental." *No Gender: Reflections on the Life & Work of Kari Edwards*. Eds. Julian T. Brolaski, Erica Kaufman, and E. Tracy Grinnell. Brooklyn: Litmus Press, 2009. 170-85. Print.

Cope, Jane. "akilah and kari." *Travelcoat*. N.p., 11 2012. Web. 25 Nov. 2012.

edwards, kari. *Bharat Jiva*. Brooklyn: Belladonna Books / Litmus Press, 2009. Print.

—. *having been blue for charity*. Buffalo: BlazeVox, 2003. Print.

—. Interview by Lance Phillips. *Here Comes Everybody*. 03 2005. 04 2006. Web. 11 Jun. 2012.

—. "let us say goodbye." *Tarpaulin Sky*. 4.1 (2006): n. page. Web. 11 Jun. 2012.

—. "a narrative of resistance." *Biting the Error*. Eds. Mary Burger, Robert Glück, Camille Roy, and Gail Scott. Toronto: Coach House. 2004. 266-68. Print.

—. "Narrative/Identity." *Narrativity*. 3. n. page. Web. 11 Jun. 2012.

—. *Obedience*. Factory School. 2005. Print.

Kilian, Kevin. "Long Ago Tomorrow." *Keep the Lights On*. 09 2011. Web. 11 Jun. 2012.

Levinas, Emmanuel. *Some Reflections on the Philosophy of Hitlerism*. Paris: Payot-Rivages, 1997. Print.

Oliver, Akilah. "Shifting the Subject: an interview with kari edwards." *Rain Taxi Online*. Spring 2003. Web. 11 Jun. 2012.

"Spiritual." *The Oxford English Dictionary*. Second Edition. 2009. Print.

BRENT EMERSON

FROM *EDGE OF A MOUNTAIN FOREST*

Sparse the distance: solid dark trees fading long away to tumble seasons out of days. The calendar betrays the sky. In summer will be autumn; in autumn, spring. Will the rain cry out for the rain? To love the worms, first love the light.

Her right: *my love is mine and I am separate* as flesh pulls from the left, her body cold, the inside of her silent. Everyone chewing over the meat of the other side: how can you have history, then splinter the brush?

The most important phenomenon will glide through accident; we shadow its face, recorded in a cup of cold dew. Days that have no work are one house, but it's only on the way out of town. The golden hour chooses days like a small stream emptying into a paper lake.

A slow light slips on stone, rings us awake. Ice writes on us and leaves every brush of sky darker. Inside the light, the morning is reflecting. Disappear our smiles into white; we frozen float along, a storm, the open silent sky.

How can I love once the wind falls? I find the humans too measured, quiet: a small house, a crown, rented. The mountain clearly hungers; behind sleeps a dragon. Horizons tongue only things much larger.

KELLY ALSUP

UN(A)

like when something you're eating
reminds you of your lover because

you like it & you like them
or they eat it & you eat them

if it's pizza even, it doesn't matter
how many ravens flock together how

loudly, the owl still comes before the weather of
What are you doing here? Why do you whisper?

It does not matter how open the mouth
It is whether you can see what's in it, not

whether you like the olives, but
rather, whether you talon

&
wing them off

FOSSIL & FOUND

each heart its own organism
a cat, cloyed belly up by its tender
kill, an impulse to conquest as well as
to feed: light-footed threads of territory
shuffling into dust, or is it clay, the draft of
wing or the space the water will always move
between, without being noticed, almost except
when it has been dry for—oh, what—a few days
& a rainstorm or seawall enfolds what once was held

by shell & soft meat will wound no more
by salt, by birth, by wave unfettered
ring after ring of music

a coral place
a red reef of gold
a silver sheaf where what is

coiled and unbound all oxidize blue
latches, hinge of spine snapped open to face
a threatless sky, maker of which this old & sauntered
sedimentary rubble assembles a ground we are known by

PORTFOLIO 2

OLIVIA LOCHER

FROM ***ANOTHER DAY ON EARTH***

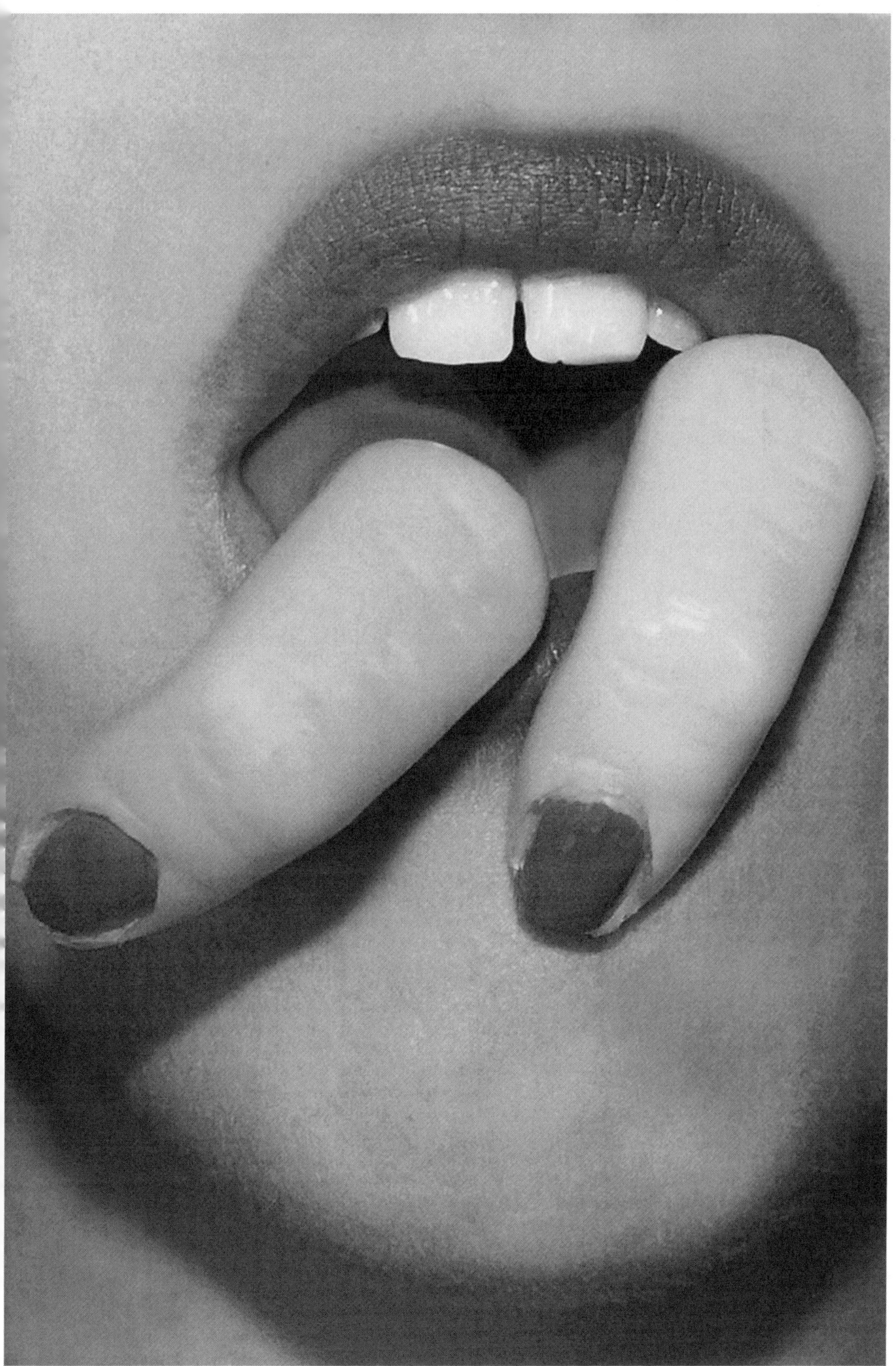

CACONRAD

with BRENNA LEE

(SOMA)TIC DISOBEDIENCE

An Interview with CAConrad

Naropa University; Boulder, Colorado
June 2012

CAConrad is an alchemist of language, turning confrontations into color and crystals into dreams. His engagement with poetics blurs the lines between poetry and reality, the mystic and the mundane. In June of 2012, Conrad taught a class on (Soma)tic Poetry during the Jack Kerouac School's Summer Writing Program. We met to discuss ritual, transgression, trauma, and the practice of living poetry every day.

BRENNA LEE: The first thing I wanted to talk with you about is Pennsylvania. Are you from Philadelphia?

CACONRAD: No, I moved to Philadelphia in 1986. I grew up in rural Pennsylvania.

B.L. Your work seems to explore elements of working-class culture and white-trash culture. I'm interested in these ideas as heritage, but also as archive and art. It reminds me in a way of Ilya Kabakov's archives of trash as installation. Or Warhol's film *Trash*. How do you think your interest in these cultures affects your own work?

C.C. I won't deny where I came from, but I'm not interested in it any more than I am interested in any small-minded group of mean-spirited people. There's nothing romantic about homophobia and racism and an inane sense of power from alcohol. Trash may be an aspersion, but it's accurate. I saw my mother arrested when I was nine, and her third husband was a pedophile, and by the time I was ten I was completely paranoid from the task of protecting my younger sister from this creep. I hate where I came from. Hate's a strong word, and I'll use it. These people will always disgust me. I grew up in a part of rural Pennsylvania where the Ku Klux Klan has a foothold. Two filmmakers from Delinquent Films are making a documentary about me, and they went back to where I grew up to interview my father. I think they were wondering if I was exaggerating the details of this bigoted little town. They asked my dad about the KKK, and he closed the windows and drew the blinds before saying anything, and he talked about their resurgence in the 1990s. In the 90s the coffin factory in town closed, a factory that had been there for over a century and was one of the area's main sources of income. The Klan feeds a community's financial fears with their illogical and frightening campaign to blame people of color. Meanwhile, it was President Clinton's NAFTA that was to blame, of course. Anyone who lived in the initial era of NAFTA in America knows how the factories all headed south to use the people of Mexico as fodder for new factories with no EPA standards, no OSHA standards. Decades of labor rights to protect workers could be wiped clean in Mexico. So, the Klan was blaming immigrants and African Americans when the real people to blame were rich white men who owned the factories and bought their way through Washington.

When I was outed in high school the town's hatred of homosexuals changed me. For me there was life before I was outed, and then a very different life after being outed. It's like one day no one will talk to you and this new way of living begins, and it's amazing when that kind of societal switch gets flipped in your life. It's most definitely a form of Hell on Earth with the ridicule, daily assaults, and the shunning. There was a bet about when I would kill myself. Junior year? Senior year? I wonder if someone bet that I was too strong for the tyranny? They were the winner! Being branded a zero gives you tremendous freedom though. In fact, it makes you freer than your oppressor will ever be because you don't have to follow their rules because you are forbidden to signify the good citizen. Unless of course you're one of those boring faggots or dykes who actually wants to assimilate. A toast to autonomy! Eileen Myles once said, "It's good to be hated." I understand that.

B.L. I had no idea that the KKK was so present in Pennsylvania.

C.C. It's embarrassing that so many stupid, mean people live in my state. At least they're not in my state of mind. Pennsylvania is one of the largest hate-group states.

B.L. I can believe that. I saw an Internet video the other day that had slogans for every state. Pennsylvania's was "Even our Amish will fight you." I wasn't sure what that meant exactly. Except that maybe Pennsylvania has a generally violent population. I saw on your blog recently that you collaborated on a shortstop animation video for *A Beautiful Marsupial Afternoon*. It's really strange and lovely.

C.C. The Italian artist Luca Dipierro made it. His partner is the writer Leni Zumas. Their collaboration recorded for *JUPITER 88* is great! [JUPITER88poetry.blogspot.com]. They live in Portland now. He was working at a wonderful independent bookstore in Asheville called Malaprops when I first met him. It's a wonderful store, and he set up a reading for *The Book of Frank* when it first came out.

B.L. Was the film an ongoing collaboration?

C.C. No. He said "I would like to do this," and I said, "I would love it if you did this!" And that's about all the exchange we had. Luca and Leni are people I wish I lived closer to, saw more of.

B.L. I see a lot of potential for installation and performance around your texts. Do you create visual art or are you particularly influenced by any visual or performance artists?

C.C. Everything can be part of the praxis. In my new book there is a (Soma)tic exercise called "Touch Yourself For Art," which is a poetry ritual for a favorite piece of art in a museum using candy, binoculars, cotton balls, etc. In 2005, I decided that I didn't just want poetry in my life; I wanted it to be my life. That's when I started creating (Soma) tics, which are ritualistic structures where we can actually be inside the forming poems. The first thing I did was eat a single color of food for a day for seven days. It was red food the first day, then orange, yellow, green, blue, purple, and white. I also wore the colors by way of red wigs, purple nipple clamps, semen, and other everyday objects. I'm excited to have been working with other artists in the last few years. Ellie Goudie-Averill took several (Soma)tics from my new book and choreographed them. As she told Joshua Beckman, my publisher and editor, wherever it says "write," she put in the word "dance." It's that simple. And now there are also visual artists using them, like the painter Jonas Slonackner is painting with (Soma)tic exercises. There's a filmmaker named Courtney Shumway who is making films with them. I'm very excited about the possibilities!

B.L. Speaking of ritual and (Soma)tics, I'm interested in the tarot.

C.C. I usually always have my deck with me. I received it when I was eighteen. They were created by the brilliant artist Penny Slinger, and they're called the Dakini Oracle Tarot. In my opinion, her deck is like a study in comparative religions, and it's an ambitious departure from the way most tarot decks continuously refashion themselves off the Rider-Waite. The genius of Penny Slinger is that she changed tarot forever because the structures weren't big enough for her, and she decided to create an entire new anatomy for the oracle. Do you want to see the cards? Here they are.

B.L. These are beautiful.

C.C. When I was nineteen, I met a drag queen named Peppy in Philadelphia. She was a New Age drag queen with lots of crystals, statues of Isis, and she had an enormous Eye of Horus tattoo on her back, which you would see when you went swimming with her. Peppy taught me to read the tarot through the zodiac to compound the information. Peppy challenged me to take Penny Slinger's tarot into a cosmic overview. Or maybe take it into a cosmic overdrive, hahaha!

B.L. Are you working with tarot in your class this week? I have friends taking your class who absolutely love it.

C.C. Yes, we're going to make our own tarot. It's a poetry tarot. It's a take-home assignment where they each make a tarot card with a drawing of a poet on one side, and on the other side they write the forces of divination or what properties this card would have to bear upon the question. We then use our collective deck to draw from and write poems with, I can't wait!

The students in the class I'm conducting here at Naropa are brilliant and extraordinary people! I gave everyone a piece of Brazilian singing quartz. And the thing about clear quartz, like the one I'm wearing, is that clear quartz can be programmed to help us do certain tasks. The first thing we were doing was programing the crystals to speak to trees and plants.

B.L. Dawn Lundy Martin gave a lecture last week where she showed part of a film. In the film, a woman digs a hole in a tree and tells it secrets, then covers the hole with mud to seal it, to keep it safe.

C.C. That's beautiful. I'll have to ask her about it.

B.L. Engaging with trees also makes me think of dendrophilia or being sexually attracted to trees and plants.

C.C. In my new book, I have an exercise for sex with trees, it's called "Antenna Jive." We human beings have such hubris to think our thoughts are more important than a tree's thoughts. We act like trees do not have the capacity for knowledge unless we cut them down, grind them up, make them into paper, and write our own thoughts on them. The truth is trees have their own ideas about this world, and we really need to start tapping into that more than ever now. Arriving at Naropa at a time when there's this enormous forest fire nearby and fifty-thousand acres have already burnt down, it's just breathtaking to hear that, to think about all the little animals that lived there. I turned on the news when I first arrived to see what the news was like in the area. They said fifty-thousand acres have been burnt, but nobody's been hurt. Whenever I hear that it gets me so angry because of course whenever they say "nobody" they mean "people, no people were hurt." But you know for a fact that thousands, even millions of animals and insects and birds are dead.

B.L. Even farm animals, too. A lot of people don't have time to evacuate them.

C.C. And trees too! And plants. So for me this sentence was annoying, that "nobody was hurt." Trauma has been made banal. If you go to my blog, there's a link you can click on called "8-Pointed Star," which is an interview series that I do. I recently did an interview with an amazing poetry collective in Buffalo, NY called Troll Thread. In the interview, Divya Victor talks very openly about her ideas of how trauma has been commodified and about how it is shutting us down and making this world far more horrible as a result. Vanessa Place has been publishing her. It's really amazing to hear Divya talk; she's a brilliant, profoundly caring poet.

B.L. During Dawn Lundy Martin's lecture last week, she also talked about the trauma body and this idea that the body is like a suitcase that carries trauma. And that the actual event of trauma occurred in the past, and so in this way trauma is temporary, it is something we can move past.

C.C. I believe some of our trauma in the United Sates is literally being consumed. Anyone who has had extensive body-work like acupuncture or massage knows that the body can release memories. Tissue holds the memory of trauma as well as the brain. I believe that animals have never been treated so badly as they are in our country. But it's not like someone said one day, "HEY, LET'S BE MEAN TO THE ANIMALS!" All of the factory farming is an invention of capitalism, pure and simple. "How can we get these animals to grow faster so we can get them to market?" It's about money, and the comfort of animals means nothing in the face of making money. In that quest for capital gain is the need for efficiency and with that comes a resulting brutality. The cruelty pigs, cows, chickens, fish, and other animals undergo with factory farming is traumatic, no doubt about it. You can't have such austere measures set against a living being and not anticipate trauma. And in the United States the level of efficiency for the time it takes to raise a cow, slaughter her, and make a burger out of her is unrivaled. And the trauma in that tissue is now being chewed, consumed, and transferred into a nation of extremely violent people. Murder and suicide, the call to arms against nations who have not raised a hand against us, we're a frightening nation! In the end, the trauma we cause is the trauma we become. I've been a vegetarian since 1988, and having stepped outside this trauma-consumption cycle for so long, it's clear to me that our cruelty to animals is evidence of our cruelty to one another and other nations.

B.L. It reminds me of the principles behind vegetarianism in the yogic diet, that you cannot live purely while sustaining yourself on the souls of other beings. The idea of consumed and inherited trauma. Do you consider yourself to be solely a poet? Do you ever write prose or hybrid text?

C.C. I'm a poet. Everything I write is for poems. Algebra is nothing more than a way to poems. Poetry is something I do on the way to the bank, to the grocery store, turning every single mundane errand into a place to find poetry. I fought hard inside myself to get to this, and I don't want to be anybody but me. Everything is a way to the poem, no matter how frightening. When I was mugged at knifepoint, it took me fifteen minutes to calm down and figure out how to make it into poetry. Did you ever hear of Short Mountain, Tennessee?

B.L. No, I don't think so.

C.C. Short Mountain is an intentional queer arts community in Tennessee. My boyfriend, Earth, also known as Mark, moved there and was murdered there. He found a cave to meditate in every morning, and he told me about the cave on the phone, and we were making plans for me to visit and see his cave and new life. Less than a week later homophobic men followed him to the remote cave on the mountainside, bound and gagged him, covered him in gasoline, and, that was it. He burned to death, and it changed my life forever, his brutal murder.

B.L. And this was in the queer community? Or outside of it?

C.C. The murder was never solved. It took me a decade to create a (Soma)tic using this tragedy to explore psychic trauma. "Double-Shelter" is the title. (Soma)tics. Soma is soul, the divine. Somatic is the body. I could think of no better way to reconnect to this man I loved than through an investigation with the soul and the body. Soma just needs a "tic" at the end to make it a body or make it a body surrounding a soul. The ritual involved methodical experiments with the home, then using the music of Phillip Glass as a trance vehicle. In the trance, the worst possible things are recalled, including all the nightmares that ruled my nights for months after the murder. Anyone who thinks it's a good time to be a homosexual is out of their minds! Especially if you are a gay man in Iraq where they call faggots puppies. How sick is it that the LGBT community in the United States is actually excited about gays being allowed in the military? Our military has created one of the worst gay genocides of our time in Iraq. Everything is making less and less sense in our world these days. Rainbow stickers on machine guns to kill Arabs! How disgraceful.

B.L. Why is this gay genocide happening?

C.C. Because for years Iraq was a secular nation where homosexuals were tolerated. The religious extremists under Saddam were furious and considered it an insult to their precious monotheistic, narrow-minded views. This extermination campaign was created by both Sunni and Shiite clerics, and there is evidence that the police in Baghdad are helping. There are posters in Baghdad asking for everyone to turn in the names and addresses of gay men. It's a fucking witch-hunt, and these men are tortured and murdered! It pains my soul thinking of the gay community in the United States turning deaf ears to this genocide we are responsible for, and they turn away because there truly is no way to negotiate being against war and being in favor of a gay-friendly US military. It's too complex, so they choose the easy solution, which is to ignore, to just act like gay men are not being butchered and killed in a country we invaded, destabilized, and continue to occupy. We cannot occupy Wall Street, but we can occupy Baghdad, and we can do so now with gay pride. The politically-correct military will receive less and less criticism as a result. I'm embarrassed to be gay. Gay people seemed to know better back in the 60s, defying the war in Vietnam, fighting for civil rights, labor rights. How is joining hands with a multi-billion dollar military industrial complex a civil right? What's civil about the United States military? This is just stupid, mean and selfish, this world we live in now.

There was an exhibit at the gay community center in Philadelphia put together by The Holocaust Museum out of DC. It was the first of its kind, this exhibit of gay men in Nazi Germany. I went to the opening of the exhibit in order to discuss the gay genocide in Iraq with the museum staff. When I was walking to the opening, I thought, Wow, this is going to be a somber opening. The elevator door opened and I couldn't believe my eyes and ears. First of all, the exhibit consisted of twelve-foot placards around the perimeter of this enormous ballroom, each one more horrific than the next, telling about the torture and murder of gay men in the death camps of Poland. But the opening, it was actually a party! It was a real party, with booze and wine and beer and lots and lots of hummus and pita and cheese and grapes and music and laughing and, and, and WHAT? How could you possibly want to eat and drink while surrounded by these twelve-foot placards? Pictures of gay men hanging by their shoulder blades, meat hooks in their shoulder blades, which the Nazis referred to as The Singing Forest, and piles of bodies, emaciated, freakishly tortured bodies. I was stunned!

But I approached the people from the museum and asked them about their thoughts on the gay genocide in Iraq. I asked them, "Since you at the Holocaust Museum in DC say that the museum exists so that genocide never happens again, what is your response to the gay genocide in Iraq? And the fact that not a single gay Iraqi has been granted political asylum to the United States even though it's obviously our fault for tearing down their secular government?" The man who was clearly the boss of the group said, "We're very proud of the fact that at the Holocaust Museum we do not involve ourselves in politics." That made absolutely no sense to me, his answer. That's when the argument was on! But then they were soon rescued by a conservative Philadelphia journalist who hates me because I'm not the family-friendly faggot he longs to be, and he says, "Are you bothering these good people from the museum, CA?" And then whisks them away for a photo op. Why should hoping people can be safe at a Holocaust museum exhibit be weird? Why was I the weird one? THEY WERE THE WEIRD ONES! I don't get it. Genocide is okay as a museum exhibit, but when it's really going on, what? What? How are we supposed to fight this kind of madness?

B.L. I really respect your ability to transgress. You're either a punk or a cop, and you're a punk.

C.C. Thank you, HAHAHA! Autonomy is the only goal worth fighting for.

B.L. I love your book, *The Advanced Elvis Course*. It feels almost light, ethereal.

C.C. That makes me so happy. Thank you. I wish everyone felt the way you do. Before the book came out the official Elvis website had my book cover plastered on their main webpage. My publisher Soft Skull didn't mention any of the queer content in the press release. They didn't mention the vegetarian content either for that matter. But when Elvis fans started getting hold of it they were freaked out. Wow, the hate mail I received! Yes-yes, I'm a faggot, you don't need to keep telling me something I already know. But to counter the hate mail I wrote out my deconstruction of the song "Jailhouse Rock." Not a single woman's name. Not a single female pronoun. Yet these men in the song are kind of frisky, hmm. It's the gayest song ever! Elvis had a number one hit that was a gay prison sex fantasy 101. HAHA! Anyway I would email this as a reply to the Haters, which would infuriate them, but at least I got to respond to their homophobia. Not just homophobia, some people were angrier at me for being a vegetarian and making the Advanced Elvis Course a vegetarian course. HAHA! Can't please everyone, never a truer adage!

B.L. So you really love Elvis?

C.C. OH MY YES! The deeper you get into the culture that is growing around Elvis, the more you can imagine how gods and goddesses were created in ancient civilization. Shamanistic healers calling themselves The Magic Elvis Club, and the Sacred Hearts of Elvis group, and so many others. There's a group from Africa using ceremonial magic to heal with the music of Elvis, or rather they use Elvis music in their ritualistic healing. In my research of sound, and in particular how sound is absorbed by water, I've come to a semi-conclusion that the music of Elvis impacts our water molecules on a cellular level which is like an opening lock. It's like Elvis had the perfect pitch to pick our locks. We're 75 percent water, so that's a lot to be absorbed by Elvis. In my new book I have a (Soma)tic devoted to this. It's called "Radiant Elvis MRI." If you ever need to have an MRI, which I did, this is something you can do with the MRI machine, the music of Elvis, and notes for your poems.

B.L. Earlier you were talking a bit about drag culture, Marsha P., Peppy...

C.C. Peppy's dead now. Poor Peppy, I love and miss her. She died of AIDS in the 1990's. When I was nineteen, Peppy went for a sex change operation to become the woman she was inside. She asked me to be the last person to jerk her penis off, but to do it by way of a magic spell, or ritual, to properly commemorate the occasion. It's kind of corny now when I think back on it, but I was only nineteen after all, HAHA! But I went to the fabric store and bought a piece of red felt. I cut a heart from the felt, and when I masturbated Peppy I caught his ejaculate with it. Then I placed the semen soaked red heart in a pot of dirt with a crystal, then more dirt, then a spider plant on top. The next day Peppy had her penis removed, and she took such care of that plant. It's like the plant was the center of her magical practice. Then one day she knocked on my door with a baby from the plant and said, "HERE, you're its papa!" HAHA! That was funny. Peppy was always radiating love.

B.L. I recently learned the term "terrorist drag," which is when drag queens purposefully do not look passable.

C.C. I love that, I've never heard that term before. The term that I know is "booger drag." Booger drag is when you're not trying to pass. I feel like that's what I do. I go by CA because it's gender neutral. I use the initial from my first and middle name. I do that because it doesn't mean anything, or it can mean whatever I want it to mean. Gender is a continuum, and that's what's great about it. Well it's great unless someone's trying to kill you because you're caught too much in the indiscernible middle of it somewhere. Fear of gender in our species is annoying, and sometimes frightening.

B.L. Do you feel like you always write from your own place of sexuality? Or do you find yourself writing from a place of other or third gender?

C.C. I don't know. I don't know how to answer that. I've never felt like I'm a man. But I don't really feel like a woman. But I don't feel LOST, you know? I feel good about not knowing, like it's okay, it's okay. In workshops this week at Naropa, we're investigating gender. I will administer reiki to each person in class. While receiving reiki, each person will talk out loud about what their poems would be like if they were the opposite sex. Then about what their poems would be like if they were a third gender, and what is this third gender. It's going to be generative, I can't wait.

B.L. This idea of writing from the other or this third place seems present in contemporary writing communities as well as different art and music communities. I immediately think of Antony and the Johnsons.

C.C. Oh I love Antony. Eileen Myles is friends with Antony.

B.L. That's so cool!

C.C. It is! They are!

B.L. HR Hegnauer, who is also teaching here this summer, has been conducting a case study on the word "and" for the past year and has invited everyone to also open a case file on a word. I chose two words, "of" and "manifest." Do you have any feelings on these words? I know that you said you didn't like the word "and."

C.C. HR is great. I love her poetry. I do like the word "manifest," in that it is about possibilities. I wish it wasn't so stuck in the gender that it is. MAN-I-FEST. Pronouns are problematic. I had a struggle with the proofreader for my new book because I use only "they" or "we." He wanted me to use the universal "he" or "him." I just said, "No, I can't do it." It went back and forth, but finally I won the argument for "we," for "us," for our shared powers. We need to transform language and insist that it have an ongoing life of transformation.

B.L. I like that in *Advanced Elvis Course*, all of the pronouns referencing Elvis are capitalized. Elvis is God.

C.C. Yes, and Jesus in the book is lower case "h." I met Freya Aswynn, someone whose books I had admired for years. But I heard she was coming to the states to conduct workshops at a pagan gathering in Virginia, so I had to go! Had to! She's the world's leading scholar in Norse mythology. She's fierce in workshops, taking no prisoners with her long gray hair, taking her shirt off to expose the entire Elder Futhark tattooed onto her chest in a circle. I asked her why she had the runes on her chest and she beat her chest and bellowed, "IT'S TARGET

PRACTICE FOR THE GODS!" HAHAHA, oh she's amazing! But I had a private rune reading with her, which remains one of the best readings anyone has ever given me in this lifetime. She said, "The runes say you're writing a book about a god, and it's a god who sang. What are you doing?" I told her about the Elvis book and that it was coming out in a few months. She lectured me for fifteen solid minutes about not fucking the book up and not letting Elvis down. She said, "Elvis is very important. He's part of the Pantheon now. YOU BETTER GET IT RIGHT!" Freya is an amazing crone! I love her!

B.L. Have you ever been to Denmark?

C.C. No, but my books have. I've been getting photos from people showing me my books for sale in Copenhagen, which makes me happy. I'm part Danish and part Irish. One of my favorite bands is from Copenhagen. They're called the Raveonettes.

B.L. Yeah, the Raveonettes are great.

C.C. The Raveonettes have that incredible song, "Boys Who Rape Should All Be Destroyed."

B.L. We have not chosen a theme for this upcoming issue of *Bombay Gin*. Some ideas we've discussed are fertility, transgression, contemplative poetics. Do you have any ideas?

C.C. I like transgression and contemplative poetics.

B.L. Do dreams play a big part in your writing?

C.C. Sometimes, sometimes. One of the things in the workshop that I was asking people to do was to take the quartz at night and program it to remember their dreams. I've also created a dream therapy with crystal-infused water, which had led to involuntary astral projections at times. I've been writing a series of poems out of those astral travels I'm calling "Going to 108," which has gone from being terrifying to something I look forward to.

B.L. Jalal Toufic lectured here last week on dreams and poetry and silence. He discussed the ideas of motionless and immobility. From what I understood, we as living organisms are always moving, twitching, breathing. We can consciously decide to create less motion, and this is the idea of the body being motionless. The only way to achieve true immobility is death.

C.C. I don't agree with that. I think that we're constantly moving even in death. In my new book, I talk about this. About how your blood is always moving and when you're dreaming the dreams move through blood. It's all movement. In death, the cells transmute themselves, there is no rest, not one second of rest. Moving, moving, moving, the soul on the move, the cells of the body on the move to be consumed and reconstituted by the world's need for life. Maybe if you were in a block of ice, then you could rest. But if you're never frozen in a block of ice, you move move move, every cell of you moves.

B.L. You spoke about intentional community in your panel discussion this week. Do you feel like you've created your own community? How important is it to you to engage in community?

C.C. Community is essential. It's been absolutely essential for me. My friends in the poetry world are very important to me. When I was invited to Naropa, which was such a gift, I saw the topics for the weeks and immediately wanted to make the workshop a community. One of the ways I've done that is through the crystals. Like I said before, working here at Naropa with the twelve people in my workshop is phenomenal. They're incredible.

B.L. I'm interested in the crystals. They seem to have an incredible ability to affect the physical body.

C.C. Especially these. They are from a particular cave in Brazil. They're called singing quartz because when you drop them they make a singing sound. I think that they're perfect for poets. They really channel song, and the body is a song. So, whatever your body is doing, the crystals are going to make that doing increase.

B.L. Are there any other particular kinds of crystals you use?

C.C. Any of them. I love crystals. Clear quartz are the ones we can program. Then there are others like rose quartz that already have a job. Rose quartz's job is the heart chakra, respect, love. But clear quartz is what you want it to be.

B.L. In book one of *The Book of Frank*, you write "there is no noun a verb can't move."

C.C. Right, so we're always in motion. The idea of a dead body makes no sense. Frank ends up with a corpse, and so his sister throws the corpse to prove the life of the noun. In my new book, I go into this too. In the poem for the piece investigating the trauma of my boyfriend's murder is the line, "never / use 'permanent' / in a sentence / containing / a noun."

B.L. I like the idea of identity as malleable, as constantly changing. That there is no singular identity. Do you feel that your own identity shifts? Or that it has always remained the same?

C.C. I'm always growing, so I'm always changing. I don't ever want to be somebody who feels like they aren't learning. I love how Eleni Sikelianos said last night on stage that Naropa is the sister college to Black Mountain. I'd never heard anybody say that before! I absolutely agree with her, she's spot on! I think she and Anne Waldman are pretty fantastic!

CACONRAD

OBLIVIOUS IMPERIALISM IS THE WORST KIND

is ho-bo
short for
something
i just got
called one
someone
recently said
“HEY your nails
are beautiful but
the rest of your
outfit is just ok”
glamor is my
great love but is
too expensive and
too much work
my beautiful
glittered nails are
my HOMAGE to GLAMOR
every time i hear an interview
with a fashion model talking
about HOW HARD her job is
walking up and down the runway
up and down
so much walking
i become very tired in my
vicarious glamor fatigue

and i must nap
everyone around
the world knows
america's real
fashion statement
is bullet holes
every single
day we
spray the
arab world
with bullets
sometimes in
the faces of
babies we
don't have
special
little
bullets
for the
baby
faces they
have to take
our adult sized
bullets right in
the middle of
their little
crying baby
faces BLAM take
THAT BABY it's
american
fashion

CACONRAD

(SOMA)TIC POETRY EXERCISE

GRAVE A HOLE AS DREAM A HOLE

—for Brenna Lee

Set a clear quartz crystal on a shallow bed of salt over night. When you wake, flush the salt down the toilet. The crystal is now clean and ready for you. Dig a hole in the backyard. Sit by the open hole with the crystal; speak to the crystal in your right hand, close to your lips, telling it you will bury it over night. Tell it you will dig it up next morning, then take notes and go to bed. (This transgressive act, putting a crystal BACK into Earth, I mean imagine someone taking a bone from your FOOT or below your heart, then putting it back for the night!! Sick, but also quite beautiful to permit ourselves this.)

Wake and write down ANY DREAMS you had in the night. Unearth the crystal, hold it in your right hand again, and ask, "What was it like down there? Was it comfortable, please say? Was it fearful, please say?" Hold the crystal in your left hand and write as fast as you can WHATEVER comes to mind.

Next night hold the crystal in your right hand, telling it you will both climb into the hole of your dreams together. Place the crystal under your pillow. Next morning write down ANY DREAMS you had, then ask the crystal the same questions you did after digging it out of the backyard. ADD ONE QUESTION by asking the crystal if she had any dreams, or if we were traveling together. For seven nights alternate burying it in the backyard and placing it under your pillow. Take notes, take MANY NOTES. The crystal will translate the way to the poem(s) with you.

ANGELA STUBBS

BLUE RITUAL

Pick an hour of the day, either at the beginning or end, and write down that hour on a sheet of paper. This paper should be folded and put into your pocket. Before you do that recall a place on your body where you had a bruise. The kind that changed colors. Write the place on the body on this sheet of paper. Think about a rainbow for at least sixty seconds. Next remember a time that your heart felt blue. Write on the same sheet of paper what or who made you feel this pain. Sit down Indian style on the floor of where you find yourself and count to five. When you breathe in, think about Rothko and his *Blue on Blue*. Understand, you too are creating art. Intently focus on the word and color blue. This will help you find the language for the words you will write next. Walk to a river or lake or pool. Kneel down and place both palms face down on top of the water. Keep them there until they become cold. When the ache from the cold moves through your hands. Take the paper out of your back pocket and read the words you wrote and place both hands back into the body of water, palms up, letting those places release into the air and into the sky. Take both hands out of the water and place one atop the other and hold them over your heart. What is the thing you want most in the world? Think about that and hold your hands firmly above your heart. After you've thought quietly about this, think about the cold you felt in your hands and let that turn to warmth that you feel in your same hands. You are now using energy to replace pain, warmth to replace emptiness. Write the word SKIN and begin a poem about things that live underneath our exterior from the perspective of healed heart, where you sit in the face of silence, where you know what it means to sweat.

RICHARD S. COHEN

PLAY THE PLATYPUS GAME

Put yourself in a dugout tree canoe, floating snuggly safe on a high mountain lake, warm in the winter sun, thousands of miles away from family and friends, untouched by needs or worries or any obligation to be anywhere else or do anything else for weeks. And what book are you reading? A classic. An acclaimed work of philosophical fiction. A "must read" that has turned out to be the worst bullshit expression of the foulest principles you can ever remember reading. More hateful and colder stone than the peaks of jagged ice that surround your solitude, marking the roof of the world. What are you to do? What have you never done before? What have you never even thought to do? In a flash of inspiration, you rip the book in two and toss both halves into the lake. Years later that minor rebellion remains a memory of unadulterated joy.

What have *you* never thought to do? Now is the time to think it. Now is the time to do it. Now is the time to rebel against classics that would drag you down to frozen depths. Be your own bad self. Play the Platypus Game. Wade belly deep in the muck of your own life like a venomous mammal who looks like a duck masquerading as a beaver impersonating an otter that lays eggs like a reptile and hunts blind-eyed, using electrolocation.

When the first platypus skins were sent from Australia to England in the eighteenth century, British scientists wondered whether they were a hoax: a miracle of the taxidermist's art rather than of god. For naturalists considered this new creature to be so bizarrely hybrid that they could not place it on any known branch of the tree of life. For them, the platypus was *sui generis*—of its own kind—a unique new species, unrelated to any other. The platypus was a paradox: a beast so chimeric, so clearly cobbled together from mammals and fish and reptiles and birds, that it had no relations. It could only be itself.

As the saying goes, "Even god has a sense of humor. Just look at the platypus." Now is the time to go down under and just look at yourself, you freak, and laugh! Take a day. Take a week. Put down this book. Explore your unprecedented limbs. Be unheralded. Be a joy.

I cannot tell you how you should play the Platypus Game, or how long it will take you to complete your turn. There is only one rule: Find true novelty in your life. Think or do something new. I cannot tell you how to play, but here is a hint: the platypus seemed so *unique* because it seemed so *connected*; to find its soul, one must exhaust the universe. When last did you hear your baby's cries in a seaside seashell or tickle your own belly by running through weeping bamboo? When was the last time a fly was your friend or a mosquito your god? My fingers fly through the internet, and all knowledge extends to my eye, but I do not know these answers. Do you?

Please. Put the book down. Play the game.

BOOK REVIEWS

SUZANNE SCANLON

PROMISING YOUNG WOMEN

DOROTHY, A PUBLISHING PROJECT, 2012

Review by RACHEL M. NEWLON

Contrary to the suggestion of its title, you will not find stories of talented, extraordinarily confident females in Suzanne Scanlon's *Promising Young Women*. Absent are references to accomplishment and success. Rather, the reader is exposed to inchoate memory and emotional trauma as narrator Lizzie navigates existence in a mental ward after a failed suicide attempt.

Promising Young Women began as Ward Six in 2004 or 2005. Scanlon set it aside for five years, working diligently for two years to craft a collection of disjointed stories. In an interview I conducted with Scanlon, she admitted that her own encounters as an immature, depressed college student in 1990's New York City served as inspiration for this novel-in-fragments. She further expanded the concept after reflecting on additional stories of women that she identified as "generally reduced and trivialized by the larger culture."

Her stories present an uncomfortable moment of realization—persons exist in society who are unable to cope with the traumas of life successfully. Her writings reflect how a sense of tragedy, loneliness, and detachment propel a desire to self-mutilate, to commit suicide, to acknowledge the voices in one's head. It brings light to the broken persons and their ability to challenge the stability of society, of community, or life. It puts people in an uncomfortable space where cliché experiences depicted in movies such as *One Flew over the Cuckoo's Nest* and *Girl, Interrupted* become appallingly real.

Lizzie's self-awareness emerges when she decides to not become a career patient. Her reflections occur after careful observations of the other women residing on the ward:

> Destroyers were not slicing their arms or digging screws into their legs for attention. Destroyers were usually already pretty much dead inside and so the cuts were an attempt to feel something...Drama Queens could cut till it hurt but they tended to do it not so that they could feel, but so they could stop feeling. It directed the attention, the focus, outward... Copycats were not cutters at all...Copycats were susceptible. Easily influenced. It came down to peer pressure. They wanted to fit in even on a psych ward. Copycats were culture sluts.

Lizzie admits that the spiritual lifelessness of the Destroyer seemed far more deadly than a true death. She nonchalantly guesses at her status as a Drama Queen but refuses to admit it openly. To do so would mean an acceptance of her attempted suicide, her place within the mental ward ethos, an open acknowledgement of her desire to ignore internal sensation and redirect emotions. Lizzie does not want to feel.

But one is left wondering—is Lizzie's unwillingness to accept a status of Drama Queen due to a close correlation of egotistical behavior, attention-grabbing, and a lack of certifiable mental illness?

> I was not a Destroyer and would never be... This followed me around. Roger reminded me of it often. He's the one who said I was a Drama Queen. But he used the word *histrionic*.
>
> My father laughed: "Well, she is an actress!"

Lizzie reflects on her experiences as an aspiring actress. In the chapter titled "Aspiring," she discloses that she played an asylum inmate in *Marat/Sade* at summer stock. She coolly summarizes the cast selections and drama department hierarchy, finishing with the statement: "It was a lot easier to be an inmate." These moments of indifference propel the question whether Lizzie is projecting a simulated persona.

Scanlon allows Lizzie to use words that are not her own. She frequently references the statements, concepts, and discussions about her as if she is standing on the periphery, silently watching everything occurr around her. This reflects an apparent loss of voice. Lizzie acts as stifled observer—someone listening to those around her, all the while desiring for someone to reciprocate. Speaking is done on her behalf. Oddly enough, the reader finds Lizzie quick to avoid or exit those opportunities of empowerment as they arrive. There is clearly a struggle, a deficiency of language to communicate her suffering. There exists this sense of hopelessness each time Lizzie shares a story that conflicts with the power of the story itself. The narrative allows her the ability to tell her story repeatedly, all the while trying to refine it, amend it, represent it accurately.

> There is a kind of loneliness that comes from being with people. The kind that is more about a recognition of the failure of communication. The gaps. Like the other day this woman came over and I served her tea and her child played with my child. The woman told me of her career trajectory, which I have already heard in this same excruciating detail twice before. It involves a broken engagement and an incomplete PhD program. Which she considers failure, having come from some ambitious North Shore whatever world. I don't consider either thing failure at all. Still she speaks to me as if I am her judge, or confessor. I felt so lonely hearing her stories, because I know they are about her and her issues and her judges and have nothing to do with me. I nod, sip my tea, thinking about how hard it is to really truly connect with another human being.

Scanlon suggests that we are all implicitly aware of how language influences our reality. Lizzie's reality is a powerful example of self-discovery through storytelling and examination of others, yet she loses herself in the story of others around her. She recognizes herself represented in this caged space but is quick to alter her perceptions, to turn away from what is obvious.

A fascinating undertone to Scanlon's work is Lizzie's desire to be accepted both within the mental ward and outside in her normal life. Ironically, she trades one reality for another—moving from the normalcy of everyday life and a condemnatory society into a confined space of psychological volatility and critical therapeutic systems. Lizzie never stops questioning her willingness to fit in with society's rejects, reflected through flash backs on life before Ward Six. It is an oxymoron of sorts. We see a young woman determined to prove herself through casual sexual interactions with unknown men both on the ward and outside. We see a young woman classifying her place within the pecking order—those she wishes to associate with because of temperament, personality and looks and those she wishes to avoid because of a "vibe":

> Don was chatty. Most from the rehab program were chatty. The addicts were generally more fun than the unipolars or even the schizophrenics but Don Reakes disturbed me to no end. I didn't try to understand my reaction to Don Reakes and I couldn't even explain it if you asked; I simply wished him ill.

Scanlon peppers the piece with references to writers such as Plath and Woolf. Lizzie sits in her room reading the texts of these other women who have traversed this culture of rejection and terms of acceptance in their own dysfunctional, unsuccessful ways.

> This wasn't like in the movie *Heathers*, which had come out a few years earlier. We watched it over and over again. It was something we did. Back then, I hadn't read *Ariel*. In the movie, *Ariel* is a punchline; Sylvia Plath is a joke. This was before I'd learned that Sylvia Plath was real, not a joke. *Heathers* made suicide glamorous but also made fun of glamour. What I remember most is the way Winona Ryder said, "I don't really like my friends." It was perfect: sexy and sad. It was how we all felt back then.

She finds comfort in her exploration, falling into yet another escape from reality. Those moments provide her with a spiritual freedom. The failures of others bring calm, acting as a form of unrecognized therapy.

Lizzie's good behavior proffered access to the psychiatric library, where she found a book about the ward: "According to the book the unexpected failures were those attractive, intelligent, promising young women who had, against all expectation, offed themselves in the years post-discharge. I knew I shouldn't be reading but I couldn't stop. I read for clues to my own prognosis. It didn't look good."

This instance is critical, as it clearly shows how women within the pages of Scanlon's writings struggle to have a recognizable voice in a world that is unable to accept their gender, their madness, and that does not have a part for them to play. *Promising Young Women* mirrors the content of the ward book—scientifically exposing perspective, stereotypes, bias, and failure.

The fragmented writing/form/style mimics Lizzie's shifting consciousness and awareness, her internal dialogue, reflection, and incomplete thought. The narrative lens allows the reader to see the limitations in the environment, the characters. Lizzie's middle-class white suburban upbringing plays out in her often prejudiced views of those with whom she interacts. From her references to the frequent sexual interactions Dread had with men to Heather, the beautiful cheerleader, the reader witnesses how Lizzie's sheltered life influences her interpretations, limits her, destroys her being. There also exists medical deficiencies—a woman is deemed ill and made to digest the diagnosis by professionals in white coats, forcing her to believe that she is in fact crazy.

Traditional forms would do little justice to this collection. Conventional methods of writing would not accurately capture the interpretations of Lizzie's life experiences. The voice is direct yet intimate, represented in a combination of vignette and essay. Scanlon's writing induces a confusing sense of eternity—the reader is lost in this place, where events perpetuate repetitiously, realistically, with no hope of ceasing. Scanlon merges pastiche and iconic cultural references about females and madness into a skillfully written piece that is nearly impossible to ignore.

AZAREEN VAN DER VLIET OLOOMI

FRA KEELER

DOROTHY, A PUBLISHING PROJECT, 2012

Review by DENISE KINSLEY

Fra Keeler, by Azareen Van Der Vliet Oloomi, makes me think of my past and of my future. I think of death and how my closest neighbor is dying next door. I think of my future death beyond my neighbor's (or perhaps before). I have so many thoughts—almost as many as the novel's nameless narrator. *Fra Keeler* summons thinking that traces back through my own memories and propels me forward to dreams of future events. It is an extended, manic episode through an unnamed character's exploration of what's real and what's true. The narrative suggests that this type of examination should be a person's *raison d'être*. While reading, I keep reasoning, "These thoughts are not me, nor do they belong to the narrator, nor the author. These thoughts are not what make up reality."

The narrator in Oloomi's book sets himself up for an exploration through his own thoughts on life and death when he intentionally buys the home of a deceased man, Fra Keeler, in order to investigate his death. Upon moving in, the narrator becomes preoccupied with the circumstances and details of Fra Keeler's death as he wallows in a stream of constant mind babble—both conscious and unconscious. He philosophizes the meaning of life events by honing in on when things happen, how time passes, and why other characters appear when they do.

The narrator in *Fra Keeler* struggles with an infiltration of illusion. At first, he experiences an onset of hallucinations when the mailman delivers a package from anscestry.com. These hallucinations soon move into a perpetual delirium every time the phone rings or someone knocks on the door. The events the narrator creates stem from his mind as both he and the reader move through the story's landscape. The surroundings become a stage for the narrator to act out his imagination and to investigate the meaning of life and death. He explains how the present doesn't exist; only the events of past and future are real.

In *Fra Keeler*, Oloomi lends regard to objective correlation and expresses the narrator's emotions through thoughts and objects. Her writing captures feelings through object obsession. The skylight in the house is the most prominent object of contemplation. If the skylight reveals the idea of nothingness, it also becomes the guiding light that breaks through all the chatter of the narrator's mind as he considers the limitations of chronological time:

> So, what a lie it is, the present, because it doesn't even exist. There is only the moving forward of events and the moving backward of one's understanding over those events. To say there is a present, I thought, is to say there is a platform where events accumulate and then stop happening so one can evaluate their effect. It is what people do, I thought, feed themselves lies the present is always cycling into the past, or transforming into a future moment.

The examination of the skylight makes him (and the reader) contemplate the existence of self beyond the physical realm:

> There are certain surfaces from which nothing gets removed, nothing more accumulates. A steady humdrum of nothingness. But then thoughts get passed around from brain to brain, so that our thoughts are only ever a repetition of someone else's thoughts. A thought that came before us and planted itself in our brain as though it belonged to us, inextricable from our being. And that is exactly what the skylight is, I thought: inextricable.

The twinkling of self-awareness within the narrator is just the beginning of a long journey toward self-realization. The narrator and I become inseparable. I cannot distance myself from him. Readers have no choice but to surrender to the constant flow from the narrator's mind and become witness. There is no escaping it. I emotionally attach to the obsessive mind of the narrator.

As the book progresses, the incidents of the past are overtaken by the narrator's investigation into the future. At this point, I still believe in time and space, but I become more aware of the distinctions, how they are either catalogued by real-time memory or by distant memory encoded in DNA.

Fra Keeler is an exploration and a performance of human consciousness. It reveals how the mind constructs illusion—such as momentary blindness—by attaching to dreams and memories. Oloomi subtly describes how lies about living in the present moment are only ideas about how to prolong death and eliminate time and space. The narrative extracts memory, conjuring words I once heard from a Zen teacher: "Caught in the self-centered dream, only suffering. Holding to self-centered thoughts, exactly the dream. Each moment, life as it is—the only teacher..." *Fra Keeler* brings attention to the present moment as being a subjective reality rather than an idealistic time warp. Oloomi draws attention to the observer of self and others by showing that it is impossible to disentangle the observer from the one being observed.

ANDREA REXILIUS

HALF OF WHAT THEY CARRIED FLEW AWAY

LETTER MACHINE EDITIONS, 2012

Review by GINGER TEPPNER

Andrea Rexilius is not writing a revolution with *Half of What They Carried Flew Away*. She is writing the aftermath. Aftermath as invocation. Aftermath as transfiguration. Her language is temporary, existing only in the present and without borders. It occupies a space between words where clouds are synonymous to clods of earth are synonymous to saliva, which is synonymous with a word, a moment, a woman, a text, a body of water. By de-creating or erasing the respectable self, she bridges the gap between united and separate and brings the reader into "the living space" of possibility.

The transformational actors in this drama, which include they, them, us, and I, are mutually united. Rexilius suggests, "They could dictate a living body or wander through it and travel abroad," and further, "They were living spaces. It was fair to say, shaped volumes. Sites. Configurations. They glowed. At this moment they were mainly sensory. A material that reorders the shape of the room they were in. It goes through them. It disperses."

These characters are shape shifters, time travelers, memories, ghosts, outward social structures, inward psychological scaffoldings, rivers, fields, and songs. These actors converse through movement—at once bright, fragrant, here buried, there savage, but always free. In Rexilius' words "they are very close and very far from objects"—energy expressed as breath, penned across the page in operatic totality. They are detail. But beware if you desire to know, if you are looking for answers, or if you are seeking to acquire, you have stepped into the wrong diorama.

Some people fear movement away from what is comfortable, fear contradiction. Rexilius is not afraid. She embraces paradox by dispersing time. Time is always now despite perception; time is open—open as noun. She writes, "They come to the open between each breath." In essence, she creates a system of being which chooses to stay in one place (form) while transitioning seamlessly in(to) another. There is no need for preparation. Time is both visible and a multiple of itself—both witness and the observed. To accept this discrepancy is to trust Rexilius when she directs us, the readers, to investigate how we normally look at the world. *Looking,* apparently, is not the same as *seeing*. In this era when separation and discontinuity (instability) reign supreme, the possibility of existing in wholeness while alone but not isolated (stability) allows catharsis.

To enter Rexilius' menagerie of characters, which inhabit the constantly shifting landscape of her book, is to surpass the long standing Socratic form of dialogue between question and answer in order to experience the words of Krishnamurti and "relinquish something absolutely false: the traditional approach." She asks, "Do you know these hosts? These analytic techniques of osmosis?" Her answer, "They are crucial. They should exist. They should plagiarize. They are always men, but this time they are women. Therefore what you are quite conscious of must evolve. Therefore a closure." She infuses content with language that attempts to absorb and reflect limitation and brings the reader closer to experiencing, for lack of better representation, truth. It permeates conscious membrane and diffuses light in such a manner as to gradually demonstrate the art of entering.

This experience of entering is a journey through the space which opens up only after all guise of respectability is stripped away. This is not a reaction, but rather a sublime departure. Somewhere in the overlaps, in the fragments, in the juxtaposition of time and space and form, Rexilius introduces us to who we are without boundary, and for the first time we understand our own authority. We learn about ourselves without restriction, opinion, or parameter—free of convention, free of censorship, and not simply acquiring knowledge. If we accept Rexilius' promise of transcendence, we emerge on the other side "glistening with what it [this promise] evokes." In this manner, Rexilius does not write a revolution. She writes the aftermath. She writes evolution.

CONTRIBUTORS

KELLY ALSUP is a graduate of the University of Oregon and Naropa's Jack Kerouac School. In addition to working in Oregon and Colorado, she has labored in Nebraska, Arizona, Vermont, and California, where she studies at Green Gulch Farm and monastery in Muir Beach. But what does she study? An excellent question deserves an honest answer: Kelly Alsup studies the features of wave, skunk, human, community, mind, and sky. The more she thinks, the more she thinks. The better she thinks her way out of overthinking, the more she knows what to do. She loves you.

ERIK ANDERSON is a poor meditator, undisciplined and unmotivated, but he writes every morning for about an hour. And he wonders, can't this be a contemplative practice? What use, practical or otherwise, is there in dividing one's meditations from meditation? A graduate and intermittent faculty member of the Kerouac School, he currently teaches at Franklin & Marshall College and lives in Lancaster, PA. He is the author of *The Poetics of Trespass* (Otis Books/Seismicity Editions, 2010).

MICHELLE AUERBACH'S work has been published in *Van Gogh's Ear, Bombay Gin*, *Xcp*, *Chelsea, Water-Stone Review,* and *The Denver Quarterly*, and anthologized in *The Veil* (UC Berkley Press), *Uncontained* (Baksun Books), and *You. An Anthology of Essays in the Second Person* (Welcome Table Press). She is the winner of the 2011 Northern Colorado Fiction Prize and has a book of poetry forthcoming from Durga Press. And spiritual practice? Joy. Always Joy.

ANNA AVERY is from Dallas, Texas and enjoys drinking Shiner in the bathtub. Special thanks to Eric Baus and John Tucker for their close edits, and to Lee Mackey, whose inspiration and studio apartment made this project possible.

REBECCA BROWN is the author of twelve books of prose including *American Romances, The Gifts of the Body, Annie Oakley's Girl, The Last Time I Saw You,* and *The Dogs: A Modern Bestiary*. Her play *The Toaster*, commissioned by New City Theater, premiered at On the Boards. She wrote libretto for *The Onion Twins*, a dance opera produced by Better Biscuit Dance. An adaptation of *The Terrible Girls* was presented by About Face Theater (Chicago). Her altered books have been exhibited in the USA and Canada. Her work has been translated into Japanese, German, Italian, etc. She has read from her work and lectured in Tokyo, London, Berlin, Rome, New York, and elsewhere. She teaches at MFA programs in writing at Goddard College in Vermont and the University of Washington at Bothell.

REED BYE'S poetry includes the books *Join the Planets: New and Selected Poems* (United Artists Books, 2005), *Passing Freaks and Graces*, *Gaspar Still in His Cage*, and *Some Magic at the Dump*. A new book, *Catching On*, is forthcoming in spring 2013 from Monkey Puzzle Press. A CD of original songs, *Long Way Around*, was released in 2005 and a new CD, *Only Imagination*, is in the works. He holds a doctorate in English from the University of Colorado and teaches poetry writing workshops and courses in classic and contemporary literary studies and contemplative poetics at Naropa University. He is working on a prosodic study of the poetry of Gertrude Stein, Ezra Pound, and William Carlos Williams, and has practiced Shambhala Buddhist meditation for many years, and it has worked on him.

DEBBIE CARLOS was born in Los Angeles and grew up in Manila, Philippines. She has since studied psychology at Clark University in Massachusetts and photography at the School of the Art Institute of Chicago. Her photos attempt to capture objects at their moments of greatest clarity: In certain light, at a certain time of day, in a certain place. The method is to wander and notice. Moments of quiet strangeness, patterns of light and shadow, minute-by-minute surprises, changes that don't happen, something askew, something exactly in place, natural and artificial phenomena are all sources of inspiration and the subjects for her work.

SERENA CHOPRA is a 2009 graduate of University of Colorado at Boulder's MFA program, a PhD candidate in Creative Writing at the University of Denver, and a Writer-In-Residence at RedLine Gallery in Denver. Her latest chapbook, *Penumbra* was released in 2012 from Flying Guillotine Press. Coconut Books will release her first full-length book, *This Human*, in Spring 2013. She was a finalist for the 2011 Dorset prize and a 2010 Kundiman Fellow. Serena is also a dancer with Evolving Doors Dance Company and a visual artist. Her contemplative practice involves relational erasures, language sinking, and obsessive thinking accompanied by aloof visits to the zoo, cold cups of tea, cats, reading, and fierce loneliness.

RICHARD S. COHEN: Last week I contemplated Kali, threesomes, blacklight psychedelia, the grief of a brother, Devachan, 4am whiskey on the front porch, where to put my nose, cold truths from a morning star. Next week, I'll contemplate architectures of knowledge, as I prepare for my sixteenth year as a professor at the University of California, San Diego, where I teach Buddhism and Hinduism, direct the Program for the Study of Religion, and write scholarly books. Here, now, I contemplate how to give myself to you with exuberant honesty; to gift you with what matters, what you deserve. This short offering is taken from my book-in-progress, *This Side of Mystery*. Every chapter begins with a game, for the book considers the limits of knowledge in relation to the spacious play of love, compassion, joy, and serenity

CACONRAD'S latest book is *A Beautiful Marsupial Afternoon: New (Soma)tics* (Wave Books, 2012). The aim of (Soma)tic poetry and poetics is the realization that everything around us has a creative viability with the potential to spur new modes of thought and imaginative output. He is also the author of several other books, including *The Book of Frank* (Wave Books, 2010), *Advanced Elvis Course* (Soft Skull Press, 2009), *Deviant Propulsion* (Soft Skull Press, 2006), and a collaboration with poet Frank Sherlock titled *The City Real & Imagined* (Factory School, 2010). He is a 2011 PEW Fellow, a 2012 UCROSS Fellow, and a 2013 BANFF Fellow. Visit him at CAConrad.blogspot.com.

MATTHEW COOPERMAN is the author of *Still: of the Earth as the Ark which Does Not Move* (Counterpath Press, 2011), *DaZE* (Salt Publishing Ltd, 2006), *A Sacrificial Zinc* (Pleiades/LSU, 2001), and winner of the Lena-Miles Wever Todd Prize, various chapbooks. A founding editor of *Quarter After Eight*, and current poetry editor of *Colorado Review*, he teaches at CSU in Fort Collins, where he lives with the poet Aby Kaupang, his two children, and a contemplative practice that includes lower b buddhism, ambient drone, hiking up the Poudre River, and cooking. More information at www.matthewcooperman.com.

ANGEL DOMINGUEZ received his BA in Poetry from UC Santa Cruz where he founded (and continues to engage with) the Omni-Writers collective. Originally from Los Angeles, he found himself in Colorado writing as if there were aluminum shards bursting from his capillaries, bruising into a collective backscatter of gray. He is presently pursuing his MFA in Writing and Poetics at Naropa University while simultaneously breathing/writing and studying the vestigial meanderings of memory—its soft, concave sites of vanishing and the residual architecture of forgetting.

BRENT EMERSON'S *edge of a mountain forest* is at once a book-length poem, a set of equations, and a love letter to experience. Structured around the layered composition of Japanese kanji, the book explores the contextual and synthetic basis of thought through and by metaphor with language. It was written over fourteen years of long, slow forest walks in India, the San Francisco Bay Area, Southern Appalachia, Korea, Japan, and the Pacific Northwest. Brent lives in Portland, Oregon.

SARAH HEADY hails from New York's Hudson Valley and is pursuing an MFA at San Francisco State University. She lives by the ocean and seriously does enjoy long walks on the beach. She often loses herself in contemplation of urban history and architecture. Sarah has two tiny chapbooks called *Eight-track Underwater* (Splitleaves) and *Cygnet* (Catch/Confetti) and poems in *APIARY*, *Chronogram*, *Flying Fish*, *Never On Time*, *The Oklahoma Review* and *Transfer*. As a member of the New Philadelphia Poets, Sarah performed in *Redemptive Strike: Reckoning the Decade* at the Bowery Poetry Club in 2010 and *In(visible) Keepsakes: A Modern Alchemical Carnival* in the 2009 Philly Fringe Festival.

HR HEGNAUER is the author of *Sir* (Portable Press at Yo-Yo Labs, 2011). The excerpt published in this issue of *Bombay Gin* is from more recent work in this *Sir* manuscript. This is a project of transgression where the thresholds between the living, the dead, and the demented become progressively less clear. However, the point is not to find these boundaries, but rather, to allow them to disappear while still being able to exist in a held place. The manuscript as a whole, as well as this excerpt specifically, is a contemplation around the word *and,* and it considers what that word might look like when expanded into a narration on humans.

BARBARA HENNING is the author of seven collections of poetry and three novels. Her most recent books are a collection of poetry and prose, *Cities & Memory*, and a novel, *Thirty Miles from Rosebud*. Forthcoming are *A Slow Process* (Monkey Puzzle) and *A Swift Passage* (Quale Press). She teaches for Naropa as well as Long Island University in Brooklyn. For eighteen years, Barbara has had a daily practice of yoga with four study trips to India; she spent one year studying pranyama and meditation with Sri Shankaranarayana Jois of Mysore.

DENISE KINSLEY received her B.A. in Arts and Letters and is a low-residency MFA candidate at the Jack Kerouac School. Denise has written grants for several non-profit theatre companies and most recently won an award from The National Endowment for the Arts. She has been involved with theater companies in New York, Portland, and San Diego. She lives on the coast of southern California.

BRENNA LEE is a writer from Pittsburgh, Pennsylvania. She co-operates Blooming Plants, and creates text and installation dealing with the body, dreams, and holes. She utlizes a daily practice of tarot, crystals, and bibliomancy.

OLIVIA LOCHER was born 21 years ago in the woods of Pennsylvania and currently resides in Manhattan. Olivia's art is grounded in dreamlands and consciousness, while Olivia herself is generally dreaming. She breathes carefully and dances very rarely. She is a dedicated practitioner of transcendental meditation.

CHRIS MARTIN is the author of *American Music* (Copper Canyon 2007) and Becoming Weather (Coffee House Press 2011). This October, *Flying Object* will serially publish *CHAT*, an eclogue with Cleverbot. It will appear on their website each day for a month with accompanying illustrations by various artists. He is also the author of *How to Write a Mistake-ist Poem* (Brave Men 2011) and the forthcoming *enough* (Ugly Duckling 2012). He is an editor at Futurepoem books and lives in Iowa City with his wife, the poet Mary Austin Speaker, with whom he co-wrote a play entitled, *I AM YOU THIS MORNING AND YOU ARE ME TONIGHT*. His contemplative practice is born out of the hypnopompic, reading, and caffeine. Whenever he has a free morning, he gets up and directly begins reading other people's poetry while drinking coffee. This inevitably leads to a response of some sort. Sometimes it's a full poem, sometimes it's a fragment, and sometimes it's just a nagging thought that continues to snag the brain at its fringes.

RACHEL NEWLON is an MFA Candidate at Naropa University. She obtained her BA in English from Metropolitan State University in Denver and is looking forward to graduating from Naropa in July 2013. She has the pleasure of being published online (*Thirteen Myna Birds, Big River Poetry Review, Horse Less Press, Cactus Heart, Foliate Oak Literary Journal*) as well as in print (*A Poet's View of Being, Erasure, Bombay Gin*). She also had the pleasure of interviewing Richard Froude on *Fabric* and Suzanne Scanlon on *Promising Young Women*. She has been married for 17 years, has three amazing young boys, and looks forward to writing and teaching at the university level.

IAN RUMMELL is an art-maker from Johnstown, PA. He is a cofounder of My Idea Of Fun, a collective of musicians, visual artists, filmmakers, writers, and miscreants. He operates Blooming Plants, a multi-media conduit. His work is also available at rubbernecking.net.

ANNA JOY SPRINGER writes about sacred and mundane perversities, comparative materialities, and the transgressive possibilities of encounter. Her books are *The Bird Wisher* and *The Vicious Red Relic, Love*, and she's recorded and toured with 90s bay area punk bands Blatz, The Gr'ups, and Cypher in the Snow. She is currently Director of the MFA program in Writing at UC San Diego where she is an associate professor of Literature.

MICHAEL STEWART writes odd, short things that have been published in an array of journals and a couple of anthologies. He is the author of *A Brief Encyclopedia of Modern Magic* (The Cupboard), *Almost Perfect Forms* (Ugly Duckling), *Sebastian*, an illustrated book for adults (Hello Martha Press) and *The Hieroglyphics* (Mud Luscious Press). Currently, he lectures at Brown University. More of his work can be found at www.strangesympathies.com

ANGELA STUBBS lives in Los Angeles and is a freelance writer and MFA graduate of the Jack Kerouac School at Naropa University. She writes with the aim of displacing the self from experience so consciousness can help shape the way she arranges language. To have an intimacy with words is an accusation she welcomes. Her work has appeared in or is forthcoming from *Black Warrior Review*, *esque Magazine*, *Puerto del Sol*, *elimae*, *Marco Polo Quarterly*, *Not Enough Night*, *DIAGRAM,* *The Collagist*, *Lambda Literary*, *The Rumpus*, *Bookslut,* and others. She is the author of a fiction column at *The Nervous Breakdown* and recently completed a collection of short fiction entitled, *Try To Remain Hidden*.

GINGER TEPPNER is currently working on her MFA in the Low Residency program at Naropa University. In her spare time she is the mother of two remarkable teenage daughters and a bartendress extraordinaire. Forthcoming publications include *Yew Journal*, Fall 2012, and*Upstairs at Duroc*, Winter 2012.